Fresh Family
Traditions

18 Heirloom Quilts for a New Generation

Sherri McConnell

C&T PUBLISHING

KU-406-561

C333627575

Text and Photography copyright © 2014 by Sherri McConnell

Photography and Artwork copyright © 2014 by C&T Publishing, Inc.

Publisher: Amy Marson

Creative Director: Gailen Runge

Art Director: Kristy Zacharias

Editor: Lynn Koolish

Technical Editors: Ellen Pahl and Gailen Runge

Cover/Book Designer: April Mostek

Production Coordinator: Rue Flaherty

Production Editor: Alice Mace Nakanishi

Illustrator: Mary E. Flynn

Photo Assistant: Mary Peyton Peppo

Styled photos by Nissa Brehmer, unless otherwise noted; Instructional photos by Diane Pedersen, unless otherwise noted

Published by C&T Publishing, Inc., P.O. Box 1456, Lafayette, CA 94549

All rights reserved. No part of this work covered by the copyright hereon may be used in any form or reproduced by any means—graphic, electronic, or mechanical, including photocopying, recording, taping, or information storage and retrieval systems—without written permission from the publisher. The copyrights on individual artworks are retained by the artists as noted in *Fresh Family Traditions*. These designs may be used to make items only for personal use. Donations to nonprofit groups, items for sale, or items for display only at events require the following credit on a conspicuous label: Designs copyright © 2014 by Sherri McConnell from the book *Fresh Family Traditions* from C&T Publishing, Inc. Permission for all other purposes must be requested in writing from C&T Publishing, Inc.

Attention Copy Shops: Please note the following exception—publisher and author give permission to photocopy pages 38, 43, 67, 71, and 73 for personal use only.

Attention Teachers: C&T Publishing, Inc., encourages you to use this book as a text for teaching. Contact us at 800-284-1114 or www.ctpub.com for lesson plans and information about the C&T Creative Troupe.

We take great care to ensure that the information included in our products is accurate and presented in good faith, but no warranty is provided nor are results guaranteed. Having no control over the choices of materials or procedures used, neither the author nor C&T Publishing, Inc., shall have any liability to any person or entity with respect to any loss or damage caused directly or indirectly by the information contained in this book. For your convenience, we post an up-to-date listing of corrections on our website (www.ctpub.com). If a correction is not already noted, please contact our customer service department at ctinfo@ctpub.com or at P.O. Box 1456, Lafayette, CA 94549.

Trademark (™) and registered trademark (®) names are used throughout this book. Rather than use the symbols with every occurrence of a trademark or registered trademark name, we are using the names only in the editorial fashion and to the benefit of the owner, with no intention of infringement.

Library of Congress Cataloging-in-Publication Data

McConnell, Sherri, 1966-

Fresh family traditions : 18 heirloom quilts for a new generation / Sherri McConnell.

    pages cm

ISBN 978-1-60705-845-8 (soft cover)

1. Quilting--Patterns. 2. Patchwork--Patterns. I. Title.

TT835.M2756 2014

746.46--dc23

                        2013027055

Printed in China

10 9 8 7 6 5 4 3 2 1

Dedication

I dedicate this book to my husband, Bill, and to my children, Billy, Candace, Chelsi, and Sean, for their always-present love and support.

Acknowledgments

Thanks so much to—

My family and friends who have been so supportive of me while I was working on this book,

Lissa Alexander for the continued support and encouragement in my quilting journey,

Moda Fabrics for supplying fabrics for several of the projects in this book,

Lori Holt for supplying fabrics and for her always-wonderful inspiration,

Pam Vierra-McGinnis for supplying fabrics (and encouragement), and

Andrea Marquez, Natalia Bonner, and Gail Begay for quilting many of the projects in this book; it's always a treat to see your work make the quilts come to life!

Many thanks to my blog readers who offer encouragement to me as I continue my quilting journey.

And I would especially like to thank all quilting bloggers whose willingness to share their thoughts about their craft is such an inspiration to me.

Contents

Introduction   4

Inspired by My Grandmothers   6

Emma's Bear Paw   10

Stars over Iowa   14

Beach Houses   17

Spools   20

Sugar Pine   24

Sugar Pine Pillow   27

Century Farm   30

Grandma's Dresden Pillow   33

Kitchen Sink   39

Inspired by Design and Fabric   45

Indian Summer   46

Summer Star   50

Spring Flowers Pillow   52

Groovy   54

Sassy   58

Garden Days   61

Breeze Pillow   64

Tumblers   68

Boardwalk Runner   72

Quiltmaking Basics   74

Supplies and Tools
Cutting
The ¼" Seam
Pressing
Half-Square Triangles
Corner-Square Triangles
Making Freezer-Paper Templates
Appliqué Basics
Borders
Backing
Binding

About the Author   79

Resources   79

Finding and Using Inspiration
for Quiltmaking   5

Inspired Journaling   23

Inspired Studio Space   36

Inspired by Fabric   49

Inspiration Notebook   60

Introduction

The idea for this book came when I was nearing the completion of the rough draft stage for my first book, *A Quilting Life: Creating a Handmade Home*. As I was reflecting on my quilting journey and especially on the photographs of the family quilts that were taken for that book, I started looking at the family quilts as inspiration and not just as a part of my heritage. I loved the family quilts my grandmother had, and I sat down to interview her about them. I also wrote to my great-aunts, asking for photos and information about any family quilts in their possession.

I thought it would be a lot of fun to use those quilts as a stepping-off point and design my own quilts based on different aspects of these family heirlooms. I studied the family quilts to see what I could learn from them. Most were made from scraps. Most didn't have borders, or if they did have borders, they were made from the same muslin as the background. Bindings were often made of muslin as well. These quilts were made to be used by the maker and her family, or they were given as gifts.

I realized that the quilt makers managed to use the fabric and scraps that they had on hand to create the designs they imagined in their minds. Even though some of the quilts were made for regular household use, each has an artistic element. These quilts were works of love, and they inspired me. This led me to think about inspiration from many different angles and to ponder where I get motivation for my own quilting. I became aware that I'm not only inspired by family quilts, vintage quilts, and block designs, but also by beautiful fabrics when deciding what to sew and what design to use. From this came *Fresh Family Traditions*.

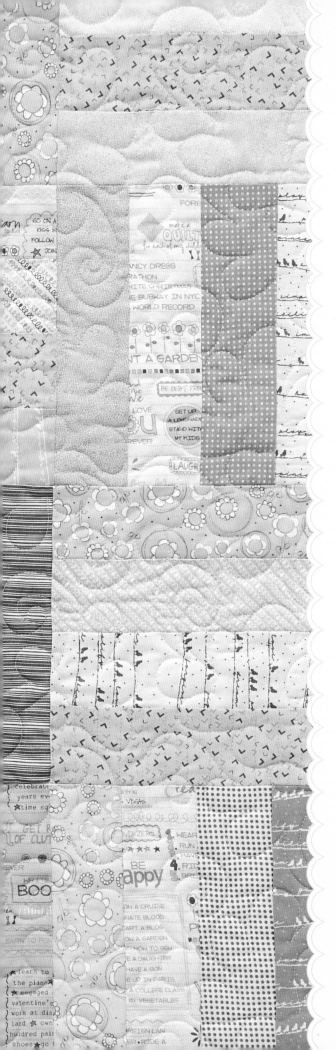

Finding and Using Inspiration for Quiltmaking

As quilters we may be inspired on a daily basis by everything around us. Nature, architecture, home décor, and even clothing influence our color and design likes and dislikes. Being aware of these influences and how to use them in designing quilts was something I appreciated learning from other quilters in various classes and lectures.

Whether you look at quilts online, in magazines, at quilt shops, or at quilt shows, there are always those quilts that instantly appeal to you. Other quilts might not inspire you. One of the best pieces of quilting advice I ever received was to make a note of my likes and dislikes in the quilts that I see. By recording this information, I was finally able to make sure that I created quilts that include the elements of design and color that I love.

Attending quilt shows and informational lectures can also be incredibly inspiring. I recently attended a quilting retreat that included several trunk shows, show-and-tell, and lectures by a variety of quilters and artists. It was fascinating to see that with every presentation, the topic of inspiration was mentioned. Every story was fascinating because the presenters were able to explain the things that influenced their designs and choices. I am convinced that all quilters are artists regardless of whether they are creating their own original designs or using someone else's patterns and fabrics. This is especially apparent to me as I teach classes and observe the fabric choices made by individual students making the same pattern.

Throughout this book, I've included ideas and suggestions that you can use to spark your imagination. It is my hope that you will use them to create quilts that you and your family will treasure for generations.

Inspired by My Grandmothers

Family quilts made by my grandmother, great-grandmother, and great-great-grandmother inspired the quilts in this section of the book. Working with these treasured quilts has been immensely satisfying.

Photos by Korindi Olson Totten

Stars over Iowa *made by Emma Acelia Wakefield Fitzgarrald*

Stars over Iowa is a quilt made by my great-great-grandmother Emma Acelia Wakefield Fitzgarrald. I love the variety of fabrics she used in this quilt. I'm quite sure they were scraps from other sewing projects. My grandmother recalls that many of the fabrics in her grandmother Emma's quilts were scraps from the aprons and dresses that she remembers her grandmother wearing. See my *Stars over Iowa* interpretation (page 14).

Bear Paw *made by Emma Acelia Wakefield Fitzgarrald*

When I finished my *Bear Paw* (page 10) and put it next to my great-great-grandmother's Bear Paw, I felt a thrill of excitement that was hard to explain. There sat two quilts of almost identical design made by women in the same family, four generations apart. It was a wonderful feeling!

Grandma Bice's Baby Blocks quilt

I have fond memories of standing on a small step-ladder in my great-grandmother's house in Cedar Rapids, Iowa, while she let me do the dishes at the young age of five. Since my mom wouldn't yet let me do the dishes, this was a really big deal for me! I still remember Grandma Bice, as I called her, stressing the importance of washing the dishes and rinsing them well. My great-grandmother didn't quilt a lot; she is perhaps best known in the family for her chocolate mayonnaise cake, her chicken noodle soup, and the net dish scrubs that she gave to members of the family at Christmas time.

Photo by Debby Leavitt

My great-great-grandmother Emma Acelia Wakefield Fitzgarrald was very fond of Dresdens. She made so many Dresden blocks during her lifetime that upon her passing, the blocks were divided between her four daughters, with enough blocks for each daughter to make her own quilt.

One day my grandmother was going through some items in an old trunk with me. Inside the trunk were three Dresden blocks that hadn't been used in the quilt she had made from her collection of blocks. Several years later, after I began quilting, I remembered the blocks and asked my grandmother if I could have them. She graciously gave them to me. I appliquéd each one to a background and bordered them with a coordinating solid border. It was so much fun working on blocks that had been stitched nearly 80 years earlier—I remember looking at the threads and the stitches with wonder. I thought much about the fact that my great-great-grandmother was an older woman while making these blocks in the 1930s, much older than I was while working with them in the twenty-first century.

I decided that I really wanted to keep one of the Dresden blocks on my inspiration board and that it might be best to frame the other two blocks after hand quilting them.

Framed piece made by Sherri McConnell using one of Emma Acelia Wakefield Fitzgarrald's Dresden blocks.

My great-great-grandmother Emma must have drawn her own templates for her Dresden blocks because they use an odd number of petals (13) for each block.

My great-grandma Bice was drawn to making a few quilts in her later years. The Baby Blocks quilt in my possession is one she hand pieced while recovering from cataract surgery in the 1970s. The blocks are not perfect, but she persevered and finished this true family treasure. *Kitchen Sink* (page 39) is a tribute to my great-grandmother Virginia Lee Fitzgarrald Bice.

Machine, quilt, and spools belonging to Virginia Lee Fitzgarrald Bice, my great-grandmother

Great-Grandmother Virginia's Baby Blocks

Emma's Bear Paw

Finished block: 11″ × 11″ • Finished quilt: 62″ × 62″

Fabrics: Marmalade by Bonnie & Camille for Moda Fabrics and Moda Bella Aqua

Pieced by Sherri McConnell and quilted by Natalia Bonner

This quilt is one of my favorites! I've long been drawn to the Bear Paw block, and it was fun to find that my great-great-grandmother Emma Acelia Wakefield Fitzgarrald must have been drawn to this design as well. In fact, this quilt, and my desire to remake it in a modern style, was actually the inspiration for this entire book!

Emma's Bear Paw was made using 16 different fabrics, one fabric in each block. The blocks are set on point, which is another aspect of the quilt that I truly love! There is no border, and while Great-Great-Grandmother Emma used a white binding (from the same fabric as her background), I really wanted a splash of color around the edge and decided to use a solid aqua for the binding. In making mine modern, I chose a vintage modern fabric—Marmalade by Bonnie & Camille—and in keeping with the design of the original quilt, I didn't use a border.

Grandma's blocks were not perfectly pieced (she clearly hand pieced her blocks); her points were often cut off, and most of the blocks vary a little in size. These characteristics truly add to the charm of this family heirloom. I designed my blocks to most capture the feel of the original and hope you'll enjoy making this quilt as much as I did.

Block Assembly

Refer to Quiltmaking Basics (page 74) as needed. Seam allowances are ¼˝ unless otherwise noted.

1 Place a print 2½˝ × 2½˝ square on a white 2½˝ × 2½˝ square, right sides together, and make half-square triangles (see Half-Square Triangles, page 75). Press open. Make 16. Trim the units to 2˝ × 2˝.

Materials

Assorted prints: 16 fat eighths or ⅛-yard pieces

Light background: 3½ yards

Backing: 4 yards

Binding: ⅝ yard

Batting: 70˝ × 70˝

Cutting

Assorted prints:
From each of the 16 prints:

- Cut 4 squares 3½˝ × 3½˝ for Bear Paw squares.

- Cut 8 squares 2½˝ × 2½˝ for half-square triangles.

- Cut 1 square 2½˝ × 2½˝ for block center.

Light background:
- Cut 128 squares 2½˝ × 2½˝ for half-square triangles.

- Cut 64 squares 2˝ × 2˝ for block corners.

- Cut 64 rectangles 2½˝ × 5˝ for block sashing.

- Cut 9 squares 11½˝ × 11½˝ for setting blocks.

- Cut 3 squares 16⅞˝ × 16⅞˝; cut in quarters diagonally for side setting triangles.

- Cut 2 squares 8¾˝ × 8¾˝; cut in half diagonally for corner setting triangles.

Binding:
- Cut 7 strips 2½˝ × width of fabric.

Sew 2 half-square triangle units together and press. Sew the unit to the left side of a 3½″ × 3½″ medium square. Press the seams toward the square. Make 4.

Make 4.

 Sew a 2″ × 2″ square and 2 half-square triangle units together. Press the seams toward the 2″ square. Make 4.

Make 4.

Sew the units from Step 3 to the units from Step 2. Press toward the large square.

Combine units.

Arrange the units from Step 4 with 4 background 2½″ × 5″ rectangles and 1 matching 2½″ × 2½″ square as shown. Sew the units together in rows. Press toward the light fabric. Sew the rows together to complete the block.

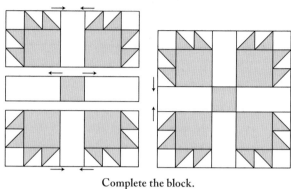

Complete the block.

Repeat Steps 1–5 to make a total of 16 blocks.

Photos by Korindi Olson Totten

Quilt Assembly

1 Arrange and sew the Bear Paw blocks and 9 setting blocks together in diagonal rows as shown in the quilt assembly diagram. Press the seams toward the setting blocks and setting triangles.

2 Sew the rows together.

3 Layer the backing, batting, and quilt top. Quilt as desired. Bind the edges (see Binding, page 77).

Quilt assembly

One of Emma's Bear Paw blocks

Stars over Iowa

Finished block: 8″ × 8″ • Finished quilt: 59″ × 75″

Fabrics: A variety of fabrics designed by Amy Butler for Rowan/Westminster Fabrics

Pieced by Sherri McConnell and quilted by Andrea Marquez

With *Stars over Iowa* I wanted to showcase some of the modern fabrics that I love while at the same time paying tribute to the original quilt (page 6) made by my great-great-grandmother Emma Acelia Wakefield Fitzgarrald. The original quilt had 50 Star blocks that are 6″ × 6″ set with 50 alternating white squares. My quilt has 32 Star blocks and 31 background squares set in 9 rows of 7 blocks each. I designed my blocks to finish at 8″ × 8″, giving the quilt a more modern feel.

The fabrics in my quilt are all designed by Amy Butler, whose fresh, modern fabrics created the perfect mood for my quilt. My great-great-grandmother's quilt was hand pieced and hand quilted using a crosshatch design (see details, page 16). I decided to use the same style of quilting with my version, and Andrea, my machine quilter, did a beautiful crosshatch design on this quilt.

Block Assembly

Refer to Quiltmaking Basics (page 74) as needed. Seam allowances are ¼″ unless otherwise noted.

1 Draw a diagonal line on the wrong side of 8 print 2½″ × 2½″ squares. Place a marked square on a white 2½″ × 4½″ rectangle, right sides together, as shown. Sew on the drawn line. Press toward the rectangle, and trim the seam to ¼″. Sew a second marked square on the other side of the white rectangle, right sides together. Press and trim. Make 4 matching Flying Geese units.

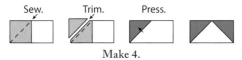

Make 4.

2 Arrange 4 Flying Geese from Step 1, a matching print 4½″ × 4½″ square, and 4 white 2½″ × 2½″ squares as shown. Sew the units into rows and sew the rows together to make the Star block. Make a total of 32 blocks.

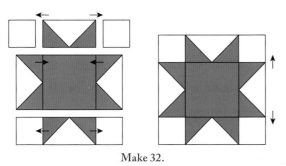

Make 32.

Materials

Assorted prints: 16 fat quarters or ¼-yard pieces

White solid: 4⅛ yards

Backing: 3¾ yards*

Binding: ⅝ yard

Batting: 67″ × 83″

* If your fabric is not at least 42″ wide, you'll need 4⅔ yards.

Cutting

Assorted prints:
From each of the 16 prints:
- Cut 2 squares 4½″ × 4½″ for Star centers.
- Cut 16 squares 2½″ × 2½″ for Star points.

White solid:
- Cut 128 squares 2½″ × 2½″ for block background.
- Cut 128 rectangles 2½″ × 4½″ for block background.
- Cut 31 squares 8½″ × 8½″ for alternate blocks.
- Cut 7 strips 2″ × width of fabric for borders.

Binding:
- Cut 7 strips 2½″ × width of fabric.

Quilt Assembly

1 Arrange 32 Star blocks and 31 background squares 8½″ × 8½″ as shown in the quilt assembly diagram. Be sure to vary the placement of the Star blocks so you have a good mix of colors and patterns throughout the quilt.

> **TIP**
>
> In addition to making sure there is a good balance of colors within the quilt, consider the print size and scale. Arrange the blocks so that larger prints and patterns are mixed evenly with the smaller designs.

2 Sew the blocks together into rows, pressing toward the background squares. Sew the rows together.

3 Piece the white 2″-wide border strips together to make one long strip. Cut 2 strips 72½″ long for the side borders and 2 strips 59½″ long for the top and bottom. Sew the side borders to the quilt and press toward the borders. Sew the top and bottom borders to the quilt and press.

4 Layer the backing, batting, and quilt top. Quilt as desired and bind (page 77).

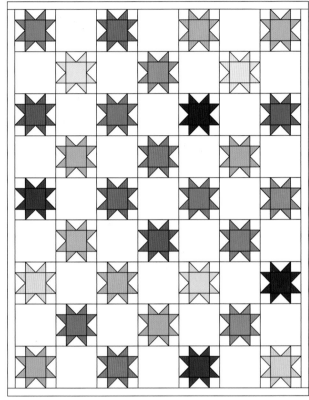

Quilt assembly

It was so much fun to have the quilting on my quilt match the original quilting done by my great-great-grandmother. The crosshatch quilting is very traditional but also has a fresh, modern feel.

Close-up of Emma's Stars quilt

Emma's Stars quilt

Beach Houses

Finished block: 7″ × 7″ • Finished quilt: 36″ × 36″

Fabrics: A variety of fabrics from Amy Butler Collections for Rowan/Westminster Fabrics

Pieced by Sherri McConnell and quilted by Andrea Marquez

Materials

Assorted medium and dark prints: At least 15 strips 1½″ × width of fabric*

White: ¾ yard

Outer border: ½ yard

Backing: 1¼ yards**

Binding: ⅜ yard

Batting: 44″ × 44″

Using more fabrics will give the quilt greater variety.

**If your fabric is not at least 44″ wide, you'll need 2½ yards.*

Cutting

Choose 1 assorted print:
- Cut 16 squares 1½″ × 1½″ for block centers.

Remaining assorted prints:
- Cut 16 matching pairs of rectangles 1½″ × 2½″ and 1½″ × 3½″ for logs.
- Cut 16 matching pairs of rectangles 1½″ × 4½″ and 1½″ × 5½″ for logs.
- Cut 16 matching pairs of rectangles 1½″ × 6½″ and 1½″ × 7½″ for logs.

White:
- Cut 15 strips, 1½″ × width of fabric; from these strips cut:

  16 squares 1½″ × 1½″ for logs

  16 rectangles 1½″ × 2½″ for logs

  16 rectangles 1½″ × 3½″ for logs

  16 rectangles 1½″ × 4½″ for logs

  16 rectangles 1½″ × 5½″ for logs

  16 rectangles 1½″ × 6½″ for logs

  2 strips 1½″ × 28½″ for inner borders

  2 strips 1½″ × 30½″ for inner borders

Outer border:
- Cut 4 strips 3½″ × width of fabric, then cut into 2 strips 3½″ × 30½″ and 2 strips 3½″ × 36½″ for outer borders.

Binding:
- Cut 4 strips 2½″ × width of fabric.

Both my grandmother and at least one great-great-grandmother made Log Cabin quilts, generally using darker fabrics. The Log Cabin quilt made by my great-great-grandmother Emma Acelia Wakefield Fitzgarrald was made using heavy wools, most certainly as a practical approach to keeping warm during the cold Iowa winters.

I love the Log Cabin design as well. In fact, two of my earliest projects were a Christmas Log Cabin quilt and a country-style Log Cabin quilt using 1″ strips. But with this quilt, I wanted to make Log Cabins that reflect some of the lighter and brighter colors available. Since I love the beach, it seemed only fitting to use the soothing colors found at the ocean and title my quilt *Beach Houses*.

Block Assembly

Refer to Quiltmaking Basics (page 74) as needed. Seam allowances are ¼″ unless otherwise noted.

1 Sew a print 1½″ × 1½″ square to a white 1½″ × 1½″ square, right sides together. Press toward the print square.

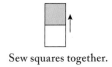

Sew squares together.

2 Sew a white 1½″ × 2½″ rectangle to the right side of the unit from Step 1. Press toward the white rectangle.

Add rectangle.

3 Add a print 1½″ × 2½″ rectangle to the top of the unit from Step 2. Press toward the print rectangle.

Add rectangle.

4 Sew a 1½″ × 3½″ matching print rectangle to the left side of the unit from Step 3. Press toward the print rectangle.

Add matching rectangle.

5 Continue adding strips around the block using the white rectangles and the matching pairs of print rectangles as shown. Press all seams away from the block center.

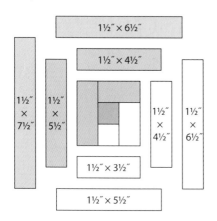

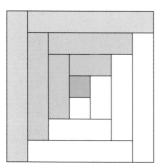

Log Cabin block assembly

6 Repeat Steps 1–5 to make a total of 16 blocks.

Quilt Assembly

1 Arrange the blocks in 4 rows of 4 blocks as desired or as shown in the quilt assembly diagram.

2 Sew the blocks into rows. Alternate the pressing direction for each row so that the seams will nest when the rows are sewn together.

3 Sew the rows together.

4 Sew the white 1½″ × 28½″ inner border strips to the left and right sides of the quilt. Press toward the border. Sew the 1½″ × 30½″ inner border strips to the top and bottom of the quilt. Press toward the border.

5 Sew the 3½″ × 30½″ outer border strips to the left and right sides of the quilt. Press toward the outer border strips. Sew the 3½″ × 36½″ outer border strips to the top and bottom of the quilt. Press toward the outer border strips.

6 Layer the backing, batting, and quilt top. Quilt as desired. Bind the edges (see Binding, page 77).

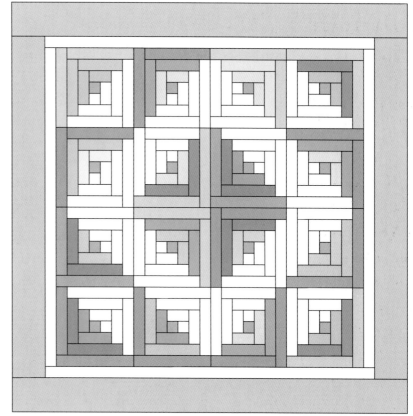

Quilt assembly

Spools

Finished block: 8″ × 8″ • Finished quilt: 36″ × 36″

Fabrics: Sew Stitchy by Aneela Hoey for Moda

Pieced by Sherri McConnell and quilted by Andrea Marquez

I'm not aware of any family members who have ever made a Spool quilt; however, I've always been drawn to them. A few years ago, my mother gave me my great-grandmother's treadle sewing machine and cabinet; it's now one of my prize possessions. As I went through the drawers to gain a glimpse of my great-grandmother by looking at what she stored in the drawers, I found several treasures that gave insight into some of the things she loved. I found many buttons, the attachments for the machine, and some small seashells. I also found several wooden spools—some with thread and some empty. Since I had already started a collection of wooden spools, I was of course thrilled to find them. I keep them together in a Mason jar in my sewing room. This quilt is my tribute to the spools that quilters in my family have used and saved for well over 100 years. About the same time I was designing this quilt, Aneela Hoey released her delightful collection, Sew Stitchy, which seemed perfect for this project.

Materials

Assorted prints: 1 charm pack* or ⅔ yard total

White solid: 1⅛ yards

Aqua solid: ¼ yard

Gray solid: ⅓ yard

Binding: ⅓ yard

Backing: 1¼ yards**

Batting: 44″ × 44″

*A charm pack is a bundle of 35–40 squares, 5″ × 5″.

** If your fabric is not at least 44″ wide, you will need 2½ yards.

Cutting

Assorted prints:
- Cut 5 squares 4½″ × 4½″ for large Spool centers.
- Cut 16 squares 2½″ × 2½″ for small Spool centers.
- Cut 56 squares 2½″ × 2½″ for middle border.

White solid:
- Cut 4 strips, 2½″ × width of fabric; subcut into:
  20 squares 2½″ × 2½″ for large Spool blocks
  10 rectangles 2½″ × 4½″ for large Spool blocks
- Cut 5 strips, 1½″ × width of fabric; subcut into:
  64 squares 1½″ × 1½″ for small Spool blocks
  32 rectangles 1½″ × 2½″ for small Spool blocks
- Cut 4 strips 1½″ × width of fabric; subcut into:
  2 strips 1½″ × 24½″ for left and right inner borders
  2 strips 1½″ × 26½″ for top and bottom inner borders
- Cut 4 strips 3½″ × width of fabric; subcut into:
  2 strips 3½″ × 30½″ for left and right outer borders
  2 strips 3½″ × 36½″ for top and bottom outer borders

Aqua solid:
- Cut 4 strips, 1½″ × width of fabric; subcut into
  32 rectangles 1½″ × 4½″ for small Spool blocks.

Gray solid:
- Cut 3 strips 2½″ × width of fabric; subcut into
  10 rectangles 2½″ × 8½″ for large Spool blocks.

Binding:
- Cut 4 strips 2½″ × width of fabric.

Block Assembly

Refer to Quiltmaking Basics (page 74) as needed. Seam allowances are ¼″ unless otherwise noted.

Large Spool Block

1 For each large Spool block, select the following pieces:

2 gray rectangles 2½″ × 8½″   2 white rectangles 2½″ × 4½″

1 print square 4½″ × 4½″   4 white squares 2½″ × 2½″

2 Draw a diagonal line from corner to corner on the wrong side of the 4 white squares and sew them to the gray rectangles to make corner triangles as shown in Corner-Square Triangles (page 76).

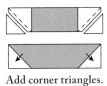

Add corner triangles.

3 Sew a white rectangle to the left and right sides of the print square. Press toward the print fabric.

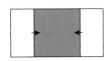

Sew rectangles to square.

4 Sew the units from Step 2 to the top and bottom of the unit from Step 3 to create a Spool block. Press. Repeat the steps to make 5 large Spool blocks.

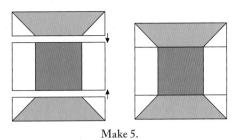

Make 5.

Small Spool Block

1 For each small Spool block, select the following pieces:

2 aqua rectangles 1½″ × 4½″	2 white rectangles 1½″ × 2½″
1 print square 2½″ × 2½″	4 white squares 1½″ × 1½″

2 Repeat Steps 2–4 of Large Spool Block (at left) using the aqua rectangles to make 16 small Spool blocks.

3 Sew 4 small Spool blocks together as shown to make 1 larger block. Repeat to make 4 blocks.

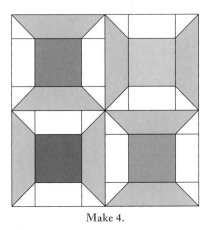

Make 4.

My great-grandmother Virginia Lee Fitzgarrald Bice's sewing machine and spools found in the machine cabinet

Some of my great-grandmother's wooden spools

Quilt Assembly

1. Arrange the Spool blocks as shown in the quilt assembly diagram.

2. Sew the blocks together into rows. Alternate the pressing direction for each row so that the seams will nest when the rows are sewn together. Sew the rows together. Press.

3. Sew the white 1½″ × 24½″ inner borders to the left and right sides of the quilt. Press toward the border. Sew the 1½″ × 26½″ inner borders to the top and bottom of the quilt. Press toward the border.

4. Sew together 13 assorted print squares 2½″ × 2½″ to make the middle border. Press seams in one direction. Make 2 for the sides.

5. Sew together 15 assorted print squares 2½″ × 2½″ to make the middle border. Press seams in one direction. Make 2 for the top and bottom.

6. Sew the middle borders to the sides and then to the top and bottom of the quilt. Press toward the border.

7. Sew the white 3½″ × 30½″ outer borders to the sides of the quilt. Press toward the border. Sew the 3½″ × 36½″ borders to the top and bottom of the quilt. Press toward the border.

8. Layer the backing, batting, and quilt top. Quilt as desired. Bind the edges (see Binding, page 77).

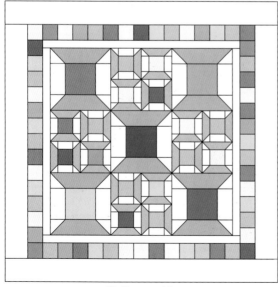

Quilt assembly

Inspired Journaling

The history of quilts and quilt journals has long been a fascinating subject for me. For several years I made quilts without really documenting or journaling about the process. Discovering quilting blogs led me to a wealth of information online but most importantly motivated me to blog so that I could journal my own quilting process. If you are wondering about what types of things you should write about in your quilt journal or blog, here are a few ideas:

- Why did you choose the fabrics? Were you inspired by the colors, the patterns, or both?

- Why did you choose the particular pattern you chose? Did you like the design, or was there a particular technique you wanted to try?

Recording the process of quiltmaking is another wonderful way to document your quilting journey. Although I have some journal entries from my great-great-grandmothers that record beginning and ending dates for the quilts they created, there are no entries about their process. It would be fascinating to know what early quilters thought about the quilts and the art they were creating. An important part of recording the quiltmaking process is to record mistakes as well as successes. I learn from seeing what I didn't like, as well as from the things that turned out exactly as I imagined.

Sugar Pine

Finished block: 4½″ × 4½″ • Finished quilt: 54″ × 63″

Fabrics: Various collections by Urban Chiks for Moda and Sew Mama Sew by Sweetwater for Moda

Pieced by Sherri McConnell and quilted by Andrea Marquez

Sugar Pine is a tribute to my grandmother Jean Lee Ella Bice Bontrager Wilkins. I truly appreciate her for teaching me to quilt, even when I didn't think I wanted to become a quilter! I remember her working on a scrappy half-square triangle charm quilt when I was in high school. She was determined not to repeat a single fabric in her quilt and often traded fabrics with members of her quilting group and guild to accomplish her goal. After she finished piecing and hand quilting the quilt, she was happily sharing her finished project with some of her neighbors when their little girl noticed two of the same fabrics within pretty close proximity. My grandmother was a little heartbroken at first. She even thought about sewing a piece over one of the matching fabrics, but in the end she decided she loved the quilt, even though it had two matching fabrics.

I decided to make my scrappy tribute quilt a quarter-square triangle quilt using many of my favorite fabrics. I did decide, right from the beginning, though, that I wouldn't attempt to have no matching pieces in this quilt. That will be a quilt for another day. I decided to use, instead, some of my favorite fabrics that had been sitting in a box for a couple of years waiting for just the right project. It was fun combining them with some recent fabrics that also had the same vintage feel.

Materials

Assorted medium to dark prints: 2¼ yards total

Assorted light prints: 2¼ yards total

Backing: 3⅝ yards

Binding: ⅝ yard

Batting: 62˝ × 71˝

Cutting

Assorted medium to dark prints:
- Cut 42 squares 6˝ × 6˝ for the quarter-square triangle blocks.
- Cut 42 squares 5˝ × 5˝ for the setting blocks.

Assorted light prints:
- Cut 42 squares 6˝ × 6˝ for the quarter-square triangle blocks.
- Cut 42 squares 5˝ × 5˝ for the setting blocks.

Binding:
- Cut 7 strips 2½˝ × width of fabric.

Block Assembly

Refer to Quiltmaking Basics (page 74) as needed. Seam allowances are ¼˝ unless otherwise noted.

1 Draw a diagonal line from corner to corner on the wrong side of each light 6˝ × 6˝ square.

Place a marked square on a medium to dark print 6″ × 6″ square, right sides together. Sew ¼″ on both sides of the diagonal line. Cut on the drawn line. You will now have 2 identical half-square triangles. Press toward the dark square.

Sew on both sides of line.

 Draw a diagonal line from corner to corner on the wrong side of a half-square triangle. The line should be perpendicular to the sewn line on the block.

 Place 2 matching half-square triangle units right sides together, nesting the seams. Sew ¼″ on both sides of the diagonal line. Cut and press. You will have 2 identical quarter-square triangles.

Sew on both sides of line.

 Trim the quarter-square triangles to measure 5″ × 5″. Make a total of 84 quarter-square triangle units.

Quilt Assembly

Arrange the quarter-square triangle units and the 5″ × 5″ squares in 14 rows of 12 blocks each, alternating the squares and pieced blocks and rotating the quarter-square triangles in every other row. Notice in the quilt photo (page 24) and in the assembly diagram that I placed the medium to dark squares in rows 1, 3, 5, and so on, and the light squares in the even-numbered rows. This creates a subtle secondary pattern of square-in-a-square units. Sew the units into rows and press toward the squares.

Sew the rows together and press seams in one direction.

Layer the backing, batting, and quilt top. Quilt as desired. Bind the edges (see Binding, page 77).

Quilt assembly

Sugar Pine Pillow

Finished block: 4″ × 4″ • Finished pillow: 16″ × 16″

Fabrics: A variety from collections by Urban Chiks for Moda and
Sew Mama Sew by Sweetwater for Moda

Pieced and quilted by Sherri McConnell

Materials

Assorted medium to dark prints:
⅜ yard total

Assorted light prints: ⅜ yard total

Pillow back: ⅝ yard

Batting: 20″ × 20″

Muslin: ⅝ yard

Binding: ¼ yard

Pillow form: 16″ × 16″

Cutting

Assorted medium to dark prints:
· Cut 8 squares 6″ × 6″ for the quarter-square triangle blocks.

Assorted light prints:
· Cut 8 squares 6″ × 6″ for the quarter-square triangle blocks.

Muslin:
· Cut 1 square 20″ × 20″.

Pillow back fabric:
· Cut 1 square 16½″ × 16½″ and 1 rectangle 14″ × 16½″.

Binding:
· Cut 2 strips 2¼″ × width of fabric.

My maternal grandmother loved to give quilted pillow tops as gifts. At Christmas time, even if everyone in the family had a gift that was obviously a pillow, it was always so much fun to see the design and fabrics she had chosen for each one of us. Coordinating pillows and quilts have always been a favorite of mine. I generally make a few extra blocks to use either in the backing or in a matching pillow. With the *Sugar Pine* quilt, I had some extra quarter-square triangle blocks left over. I trimmed the blocks down a little to make them a better size for a smaller project and made a matching pillow.

Block Assembly

Refer to Quiltmaking Basics (page 74) as needed. Seam allowances are ¼″ unless otherwise noted.

1 Draw a diagonal line from corner to corner on the wrong side of each light 6″ × 6″ square.

2 Place a marked square on a medium to dark print 6″ × 6″ square, right sides together. Sew ¼″ on both sides of the diagonal line. Cut on the drawn line. Press toward the dark. You will now have 2 identical half-square triangles.

Sew on both sides of line.

3 Draw a diagonal line on the wrong side of a half-square triangle. The line should be perpendicular to the sewn line on the block.

4 Place 2 matching half-square triangle units right sides together, nesting the seams. Sew ¼″ on both sides of the diagonal line. Cut and press. You will have 2 identical quarter-square triangles.

Sew on both sides of line.

5 Trim the quarter-square triangles to measure 4½″ × 4½″. Make a total of 16 quarter-square triangle blocks.

6 Sew the blocks together in 4 rows of 4 blocks each. Alternate the pressing direction for each row so that the seams will nest when the rows are sewn together.

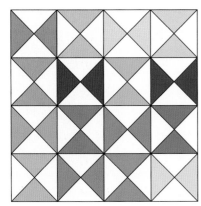

Pillow top assembly

Pillow Assembly

1 Place the batting on the muslin. Center the pillow top right side up on the batting and hand or machine quilt as desired.

2 Trim the batting and muslin even with the edges of the pillow top.

3 Make the pillow back by folding in and pressing ¼″ on one 16½″ edge of each pillow back rectangle. Fold again, press, and sew to create a finished edge.

4 Turn the hemmed edges under 2″, wrong sides of the fabric together, and press.

5 Place the smaller pillow back rectangle on top of the completed pillow top, wrong sides together, and pin. Place the second pillow back rectangle on top of this unit and pin. The pillow back sections should overlap each other. Baste around the edges of the pillow sections with a scant ¼″ seam. The area in the back where the pillow back sections overlap will allow you to insert the pillow form into the pillow.

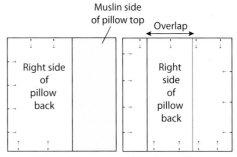

Pin and baste top and back together.

6 Bind the edges of the pillow (see Binding, page 77). Insert the pillow form.

I machine quilted these wavy lines using my regular home machine.
This style of machine quilting is an easy technique that is perfect for beginners.

Century Farm

Finished block: 8″ × 8″ • Finished quilt: 59″ × 67″

Fabrics: Notebook by Sweetwater for Moda and Moda Bella Solids in Gray

Pieced by Sherri McConnell and quilted by Gail Begay

Century Farm was inspired by my maternal grandmother, Jean Lee Ella Bice Bontrager Wilkins. Although she was an award-winning quilter who loved to piece and appliqué with precision, my grandmother also loved the Rail Fence block. She often used this block to make placemats for her own table and to give as gifts. I, too, was drawn to this block as a beginning quilter. When I first began quilting, I made Rail Fence placemats for Christmas gifts for family members one year.

In 1985 my grandmother and her sisters were awarded the Century Farm designation for their 80 acres of Iowa farmland originally purchased by their paternal great-grandparents. This quilt is a tribute to that farm heritage as well as my grandmother's love of the Rail Fence block.

Materials

Assorted prints: 1 layer cake (42 squares 10″ × 10″) or 3 yards total

Inner border: ⅓ yard

Outer border: 1⅛ yards

Backing: 4 yards

Binding: ⅝ yard

Batting: 67″ × 75″

Cutting

Assorted prints:
- From each of 35 layer cake squares, cut 4 strips 2½″ × 10″ (140 total).
- From each of 7 layer cake squares, cut 1 square 8½″ × 8½″ (7 total).

Inner border:
- Cut 6 strips 1½″ × width of fabric.

Outer border:
- Cut 7 strips 5″ × width of fabric.

Binding:
- Cut 7 strips 2½″ × width of fabric.

Block Assembly

Refer to Quiltmaking Basics (page 74) as needed.
Seam allowances are ¼″ unless otherwise noted.

1 Arrange the 2½″ × 10″ strips in 35 groups of 4 strips each. Sew each set together, pressing the seams in one direction.

Make 35.

2 Trim each block to measure 8½″ × 8½″.

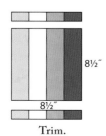

8½″

8½″

Trim.

Quilt Assembly

1 Arrange the pieced blocks and 8½″ × 8½″squares in 7 rows of 6 blocks each.

2 Sew the blocks in each row together. Alternate the pressing direction for each row so that the seams will nest when the rows are sewn together. Sew the rows together. Press toward the bottom of the quilt.

3 Piece the 1½″-wide inner border strips for length; then cut into 2 strips 1½″ × 56½″ for left and right sides and sew to the sides of the quilt. Press toward the inner border. Cut 2 strips 1½″ × 50½″ for the top and bottom inner borders. Sew to the quilt and press toward the inner border strips.

4 Piece the 5″-wide outer border strips together for length; then cut into 2 strips 5″ × 58½″ for left and right outer borders. Sew to the sides of the quilt and press toward the outer border. Cut 2 strips 5″ × 59½″ for the top and bottom borders. Sew to the quilt and press toward the outer border strips.

5 Layer the backing, batting, and quilt top. Quilt as desired. Bind the edges (see Binding, page 77).

Quilt assembly

Grandma's Dresden Pillow

Finished block: 14″ × 14″ • Finished pillow: 14″ × 14″

Fabrics: Simply Color by V & Co. for Moda, Half Moon Modern by Moda,
Happy Go Lucky by Bonnie & Camille for Moda, Notting Hill by Joel Dewberry for FreeSpirit Fabrics,
Henna Prints by Sandi Henderson for Michael Miller, Metro Living Circles by Robert Kaufman,
Bella Moda Solids Robin's Egg Blue

Pieced and hand quilted by Sherri McConnell

Since I never made the pillows I wanted to make using Great-Great-Grandmother Emma Acelia Wakefield Fitzgarrald's Dresden blocks, my tribute to her Dresden blocks is this modern Dresden pillow, using a similar rounded Dresden that Emma used in her blocks.

Materials

Assorted prints: 16 charm squares (5″ × 5″) or ⅓ yard total

Blue solid: 5″ × 5″ square

White solid: ½ yard

Muslin: ½ yard

Pillow back: ½ yard

Binding: ¼ yard

Batting: 18″ × 18″

Pillow form: 14″ × 14″

Template material: Freezer paper for making templates *or* Marti Michell's Dresden Plate acrylic templates for 12″ Dresden

Other notions:

Spray starch

Small, inexpensive paintbrush

Cutting

Make your own freezer-paper templates (Making Freezer-Paper Templates, page 76), using the Dresden and Circle patterns (page 38), or use purchased templates.

Assorted prints:
- Cut 16 Dresden blades.

Blue solid:
- Cut 1 circle ¼″ to ⅜″ larger than template on all sides.

White solid:
- Cut 1 square 16″ × 16″.

Muslin:
- Cut 1 square 18″ × 18″.

Pillow back fabric:
- Cut 1 square 14½″ × 14½″ and 1 rectangle 12″ × 14½″.

Binding:
- Cut 2 strips 2¼″ by width of fabric.

TIPS

- When cutting around the templates, use a small rotary cutter to more easily cut around the curves. You can also trace around the curved part of the template, remove the template, and then use the rotary cutter or scissors to finish cutting each blade.

- If your center circle fabric is light, cut another circle from muslin the exact size of the template. Slip this muslin circle inside the pressed edges of your center circle before appliquéing it to the pillow. That will prevent the bottoms of the Dresden blades from showing through the front of the center circle.

- If you do a lot of appliqué, you might like a set of Karen Kay Buckley's Perfect Circles. They are very helpful and eliminate the need to make freezer-paper templates.

Block Assembly

Refer to Quiltmaking Basics (page 74) as needed. Seam allowances are ¼″ unless otherwise noted.

1 Use the pattern (page 38) to make a pressing template from 2 layers of freezer paper (see Making Freezer-Paper Templates, page 76). Press the template to the wrong side of a Dresden blade.

2 Spray a little of the spray starch into a small cup. With the paintbrush, paint the rounded edges with spray starch. Using the tip of your iron or a small craft iron, press the rounded Dresden edges over the freezer-paper template. When cool, remove the template and press the Dresden blade.

Press edges over template.

3 Repeat Step 2 for each of the 16 Dresden blades.

4 Sew the blades together in pairs. It is important that the rounded edges meet, so begin sewing at the outer edge.

Begin here.

Sew blades together.

5 Continue sewing until all the blades are sewn together in pairs. Sew the pairs together in a circle.

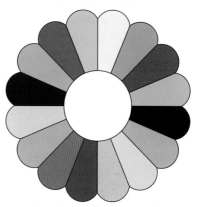

Complete the Dresden circle.

6 Make a circle template using 2 layers of freezer paper, or use the one you made for cutting. Repeat Step 2 to press the edges of the center circle over the template.

7 Appliqué (page 76) the Dresden blades and the center circle to the background. Press and trim the background to 14½″ × 14½″, making sure the appliqué is centered.

Appliqué to background.

Pillow Assembly

To complete the pillow, follow the instructions for Pillow Assembly, Steps 1–6 (page 29), for the Sugar Pine Pillow.

Inspired Studio Space

I've sewn in many spaces over the years. As a young girl, I was blessed to have a sewing machine and cabinet in my room. I stored my fabric in my closet in a couple of boxes, and I had a large sewing bin for notions and a small sewing basket for my hand-sewing supplies.

As an adult, I sewed for many years either on the dining room table or in my bedroom. Fabrics were often stored in bins in a utility closet. Everything was either out on the table or all put away. It was quite a task to begin something new, since all of my supplies had to be pulled out (and sometimes put away) with each project. It wasn't until I had been sewing for about 20 years that I finally had a shared sewing space as part of our home office. A few years after that, I was able to have a room dedicated just for sewing and quilting.

Recently I was able to do a little redecorating and reorganizing in my sewing studio. It was a lot of fun. I chose a light aqua color that inspires me for the walls. I took every bit of fabric out before bringing it back in—I organized precuts together on the shelf, but I divided all of the rest of my fabrics by color. This was quite a bit of work, but very much worth it. For example, organizing my fabrics by color let me see which colors I had more or less of. I've never thought of myself as a big pink fan, but I found I had more pink than any other color in my stash. I organized scraps by color separately from fat quarters; pieces larger than ¼ yard were also organized by color.

Along with this studio organization, I made a point to keep the tools I use most in plain sight and to keep more open spaces in the room. I sorted tools and notions by their specific use. For example, all fasteners, such as zippers, snaps, Velcro, and buttons, are in one area of the storage drawers. I actually took out a couple of shelves to create a more open look. I decided having this open feeling would be more beneficial than having a little more storage.

I decorated the room with some of my favorite quilts and color combinations. I hung my inspiration board right above my sewing machine and moved a homey quilt rack into one of the corners. My quilt studio is now an inspiring place to sew and create. It's not always perfectly neat, but I do have it organized now, so I can find everything I need quickly and easily.

A. Sewing area

B. Sewing room quilt rack—by making space to store some of my favorite quilts, the room reflects the quilts I love to make.

C. Sewing room storage shelf and quilt rack

D. Sewing room notions table—for me having the most frequently used items out in the open helps me to stay organized.

E. Sewing room fabric

F. Sewing room fabric storage—organizing my fabrics by color was a terrific idea. Not only was I able to see which colors I need to stock up on, but I was also able to see which types of fabrics I had purchased.

Photos by Korindi Olson Totten

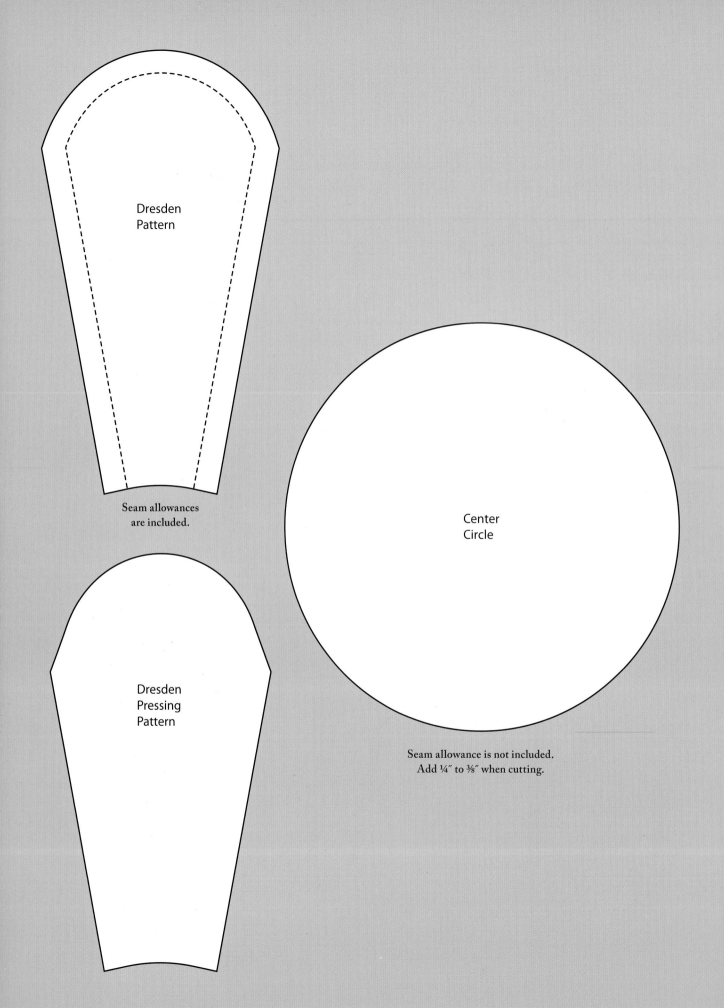

Dresden
Pattern

Seam allowances
are included.

Center
Circle

Dresden
Pressing
Pattern

Seam allowance is not included.
Add ¼″ to ⅜″ when cutting.

Kitchen Sink

Finished hexagon block: 5¼″ × 6″ • Finished quilt: 30″ × 34″

Fabrics: A variety from collections by Lori Holt of Bee in My Bonnet and
The Simple Life by Tascha Noel for Riley Blake

Pieced by Sherri McConnell and quilted by Natalia Bonner

Materials

Assorted prints: 2 yards total

Backing: 1⅛ yards

Binding: ⅓ yard

Batting: 38″ × 42″

Template material: Stiff cardboard, template plastic, *or* Marti Michell Perfect Patchwork Templates Set H Large Hexagon acrylic templates

TIP

If you make your own templates, use stiff cardboard or template plastic. My favorite cardboard for templates is the heavyweight cardboard that comes on the bottom of layer cake precuts. I use a dull rotary cutter and an acrylic ruler to cut templates from this cardboard.

Punch small holes in the templates (about 1/16″ diameter) at the ¼″ seam intersections to make it easy to mark the dots on your fabric.

Cutting

Make your own templates using the patterns (page 43), or use purchased acrylic templates.

Assorted prints:

• Cut 126 diamonds.

• Cut 7 half-hexagons.

Binding:

• Cut 2 strips 2½″ × width of fabric.

Kitchen Sink is an homage to my great-grandmother Virginia Lee Fitzgarrald Bice based on her Baby Blocks quilt (pages 7–9). My great-grandmother used scraps of all kinds—mixing both lightweight cottons and heavier-weight cottons—for her quilt, which measures 78″ × 92″. Her Baby Blocks quilt was hand pieced and hand quilted (see details, page 42).

Block Assembly

Refer to Quiltmaking Basics (page 74) as needed. Seam allowances are ¼″ unless otherwise noted.

1 Using a pencil, mark dots at the ¼″ intersections on the wrong side of all the cut pieces.

2 Sew 2 diamonds together, beginning and ending the stitching exactly on the marked dots, and backstitching at each end to secure the stitches. Do not press the seams yet.

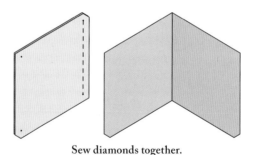

Sew diamonds together.

3 Sew a third diamond to one of the diamonds from Step 2 as shown. Begin and end the stitching on the marked dots. Sew the second seam of the third diamond. Begin and end the stitching on the marked dots. The 3 diamonds form a hexagon.

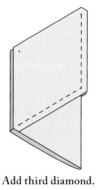

Add third diamond.

TIP

Be very careful not to sew past the marked dots. If your block has puckers, you might need to check the back and pick out any stitches that extend into the seam allowance.

4 Press the seams counterclockwise. The center where the seams meet will open flat with 3 tiny diamonds creating a miniature hexagon shape in the center. Make a total of 42 hexagon blocks.

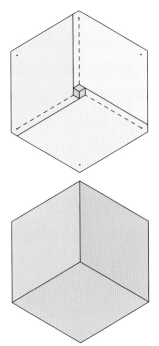

Press seams. Make 42.

Quilt Assembly

1 Arrange the hexagons in 7 columns of 6 hexagon blocks each. Place a half-hexagon at the top or bottom of each column as indicated in the quilt assembly diagram (page 42).

2 Sew the hexagons and half-hexagons in each column together along the top and bottom flat sides, beginning and ending the stitching on the marked dots.

3 Sew the columns together, one at a time. As you join each hexagon from one column to the adjoining piece on the other column, sew as before, beginning and ending the stitching on the marked dots.

---- **TIP** ----

Sewing using this dot-to-dot method is a little time-consuming, but if you go slowly and carefully, it will yield perfect results. Use silk pins to keep your pieces aligned.

4 Continue to sew the columns together until the quilt top is pieced.

5 Press the quilt top well.

6 Using a long acrylic ruler, trim the uneven left and right sides. You will be cutting off 1½″ from the widest parts of each side to create a rectangular quilt top.

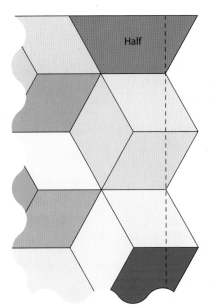

Half

Trim the sides.

---- **TIP** ----

Trimming: When trimming quilt edges with your ruler and rotary cutter, be sure that the top of the acrylic ruler is even with the top of the quilt. Check farther down in the quilt to make sure that the straight lines of the ruler are still straight with seams in the quilt.

7 Staystitch ⅛″ around the entire quilt top to prevent stretching and fraying.

8 Layer the backing, batting, and quilt top. Quilt as desired. Bind the edges (see Binding, page 77).

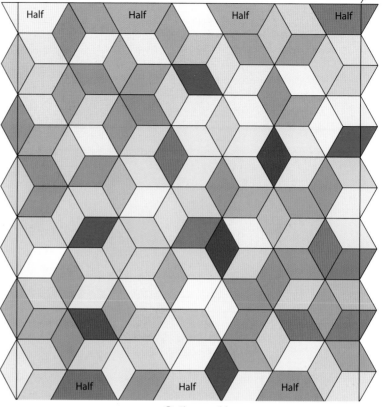

Trim off.

Half   Half   Half   Half

Half   Half   Half

Quilt assembly

Great-Grandmother Virginia's Baby Blocks

I made sure to have this project quilted in the same manner as my great-grandmother's quilt. Outline quilting ¼″ inside each diamond shape is the perfect way to quilt this design, and it allows the scrappy fabrics to shine.

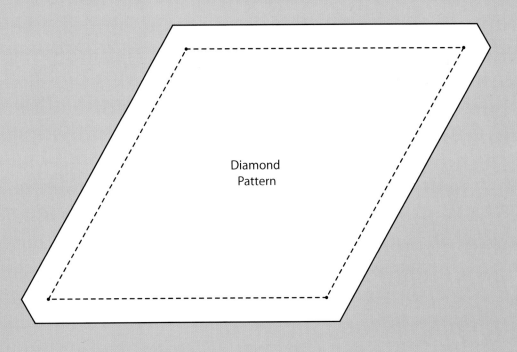

Diamond
Pattern

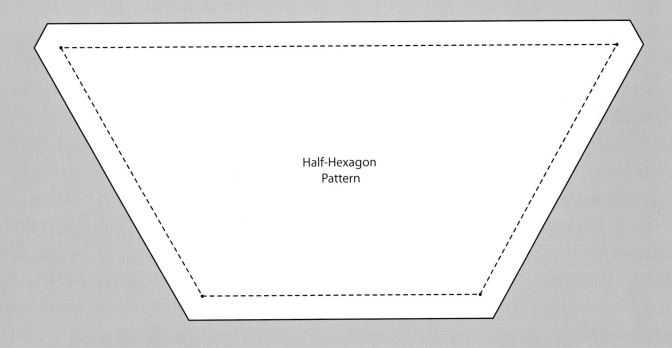

Half-Hexagon
Pattern

Inspired by Design and Fabric

So many different things provide the stimulus for the quilts I make. Sometimes I see a pattern or block that I want to re-create, while at other times I am drawn to a particular fabric or group of fabrics. Sometimes prints and patterns found in clothing and home accessories provide a jumping-off point. Stunning architecture and nature also provide ideas for quilts—there is inspiration to be found all around.

I find I'm most particularly inspired by quilt blocks, the designs they make when set together, and by fabrics themselves. When asked which comes first, the fabric or the pattern, I would have to respond both—but at different times. Some of the projects in this section have also been inspired by my desire to use up every bit of a precut fabric collection. Although my grandmothers never had the luxury of these precut fabrics, precut strips, squares, and bundles can save today's quilters a lot of time.

45

Indian Summer

Finished block: 10″ × 10″ • Finished quilt: 73″ × 73″

Fabrics: Chicopee by Denyse Schmidt for FreeSpirit Fabrics

Pieced by Sherri McConnell and quilted by Andrea Marquez

Indian Summer was one of those quilts inspired by the fabrics. The Chicopee collection by Denyse Schmidt has so much of what I love—bold designs, retro colorings, and modern style. I wanted to use a traditional block I liked (New Album block) to accentuate the fabrics themselves. After making the blocks and pondering a layout, I found that setting the blocks on point was the most effective way to present them. See Inspired by Fabric (page 49).

Block Assembly

Refer to Quiltmaking Basics (page 74) as needed. Seam allowances are ¼″ unless otherwise noted.

For each block you will need 1 print center square (4″ × 4″), 4 matching print rectangles (3″ × 5½″) from a different print, 4 cream corner squares (3″ × 3″), and 4 cream triangles.

TIP

When making a quilt with different fabric combinations in each block, I like to choose all the combinations before sewing a single block. This enables me to preview the pairings and swap fabrics as needed, so that I have the very best mix to showcase each fabric.

---

1 Sew 2 cream triangles to opposite sides of the print 4″ × 4″ square. Press toward the cream fabric. Sew the remaining 2 triangles to the remaining sides of the square. Press toward the cream fabric. Make sure the unit measures 5½″ × 5½″.

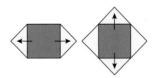

Sew triangles to square.

2 Sew 2 print 3″ × 5½″ rectangles to the left and right sides of the unit from Step 2. Press toward the print rectangles.

Add rectangles.

Materials

Assorted prints: ⅛ yard each of 25 different prints (or fat eighths)

Medium print: ¼ yard

Cream solid: 4½ yards

Backing: 4½ yards

Binding: ⅔ yard

Batting: 81″ × 81″

Cutting

25 Assorted prints:
- Cut 1 square 4″ × 4″ and 4 rectangles 3″ × 5½″ from each for blocks.

Medium print:
- Cut 40 squares 2″ × 2″ for sashing squares.

Cream solid:
- Cut 8 strips 3″ × width of fabric; subcut into 100 squares 3″ × 3″ for corner squares.

- Cut 5 strips 3⅜″ × width of fabric; subcut into 50 squares 3⅜″ × 3⅜″. Cut each square diagonally to make 100 triangles for block centers.

- Cut 64 rectangles 2″ × 10½″ for sashing.

- Cut 3 squares 17¾″ × 17¾″; cut each diagonally twice to make 12 setting triangles.

- Cut 2 squares 10½″ × 10½″; cut each diagonally once to make 4 corner triangles.

- Cut 8 strips 3½″ × width of fabric for the border.

Binding:
- Cut 8 strips 2½″ × width of fabric.

3 Sew a cream 3″ × 3″ corner square to each end of the remaining print rectangles. Press toward the rectangles. Make 2.

Sew squares to rectangles.

4 Sew the units from Steps 2 and 3 together as shown to make the block. Repeat the steps to make 25 blocks.

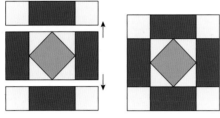

Make 25.

Quilt Assembly

1 Arrange the blocks, sashing strips, sashing squares, setting triangles, and corner triangles in diagonal rows as shown in the quilt assembly diagram (above right).

2 Sew the sashing strips and blocks together into rows. Press seam allowances toward the sashing.

3 Sew the sashing strips to the sashing squares in rows. Press seam allowances toward the sashing strips.

4 Sew sashing rows to the block rows as shown in the diagram. Then sew the side setting triangles to the ends of the block rows. Press toward the sashing. The corner triangles will be added after all the rows are sewn together.

5 Sew the rows together, pressing seams toward the sashing rows. It's easier to sew a group of 3 rows together and a group of 4 rows together. Then sew the 2 groups together. Add the corner triangles last.

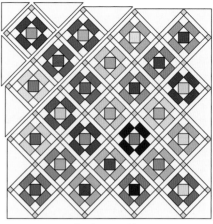

Quilt assembly

6 Trim and square up the sides, top, and bottom of the quilt, leaving ¼″ beyond the sashing squares on each side. This is easiest to do by using a long acrylic ruler (refer to the trimming tip, page 41).

7 Piece the 3½″ border strips together into one long length. Measure the length of your quilt through the center and cut 2 strips for the left and right borders. Sew to the quilt and press toward the borders.

8 Measure the width of your quilt through the center, including the side borders, and cut 2 strips to that length for the top and bottom borders. Sew the borders to the top and bottom of the quilt. Press toward the borders.

9 Layer the backing, batting, and quilt top. Quilt as desired. Bind the edges (see Binding, page 77).

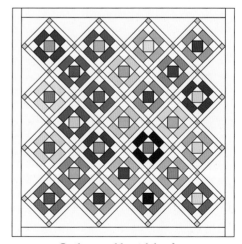

Quilt assembly with borders

Inspired by Fabric

Color

Being influenced by color is a part of everyday life. We all see and react to colors on a daily basis. Color is used by the media, advertisers, and all types of manufacturers to sway our decisions about the purchases we make. We decorate our homes with the colors we love. We generally dress in colors we love. And we make quilts in the colors we love.

Having a good idea of the colors and color combinations we like in our quilts can help us make quilts that are always pleasing. It's also a good thing to step out of our comfort zone from time to time and experiment with colors we might not normally use. Several years ago, I was beginning to be drawn to brighter colors, and yet I felt I had to continue to work only on projects that matched my home décor. When I finally allowed myself to create with colors I was drawn to, I was happier with my quilts and creations.

Contrast and Scale

Do you love large-scale prints, or is your fabric stash full of small- and medium-scale prints? Just as there needs to be contrast between colors in quilts, there also needs to be contrast between the scale of the prints you use. Large-scale prints are more striking when used in combination with smaller prints. Small prints can also stand out more when used in combination with prints of varying sizes. Placement of prints of different scale is important too; there should be a good mixture throughout the quilt of prints of all sizes. Not only should there be contrast in scale, but you should also be aware of the contrast between soothing and busy prints, and between florals and geometric designs. I love to use a variety of geometric prints; however, my favorite way to use them is to combine them with floral fabrics. As you view other quilts and make your own, note the print combinations that excite you the most.

Prints and Patterns

Which prints and patterns most awaken your creative spirit? I love polka dots and hexagons, so any time I see a fabric or a quilt design with these elements, I'm drawn to it. The polka dots say "carefree days" to me, and the hexagons remind me of quilts of days gone by. I'm galvanized by modern prints and patterns as well as traditional ones. I love diamonds and flowers, and I tend to gravitate to these shapes again and again. I've particularly enjoyed studying the prints and patterns in my family quilts. The only photos I have of these quilters are black-and-white photos, but I can gather information about who they were and what they loved by looking at the fabrics used in their quilts.

Summer Star

Finished block: 14″ × 14″ • Finished quilt: 32″ × 32″

Fabrics: Simply Color by V & Co. for Moda and Cuzco by Kate Spain for Moda

Pieced by Sherri McConnell and quilted by Natalia Bonner

Star blocks are some of my favorites, and I've long wanted to make a bright, bold star to hang in my quilting studio. The gorgeous tones of Simply Color and Cuzco fabrics seemed the perfect choice to make this quilt. Although the individual blocks do not create a star motif, when set together, the four blocks make a lovely radiating star design.

Block Assembly

Refer to Quiltmaking Basics (page 74) as needed. Seam allowances are ¼" unless otherwise noted.

1 Place a print 4½" × 4½" square with a white 4½" × 4½" square, right sides together, and make half-square triangle units (page 75). Press the squares open. Trim the units to 4" × 4". Make 40.

Make 40.

2 Arrange 3 white and 3 print 4" × 4" squares with 10 half-square triangle units as shown. Sew the units into rows and press the seams in opposite directions from row to row. Sew the rows together. Wait to press the row seams until after you have arranged the blocks.

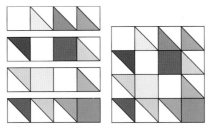

Make 4 blocks.

Quilt Assembly

1 Arrange 4 blocks as shown in the quilt assembly diagram. Press the seam allowances of the blocks so that they will nest together. Sew the blocks together.

2 Sew the 2½" × 28½" borders to the left and the right sides of the quilt. Press toward the border. Sew the 2½" × 32½" borders to the top and the bottom of the quilt. Press toward the border.

3 Layer the backing, batting, and quilt top. Quilt as desired. Bind the edges (see Binding, page 77).

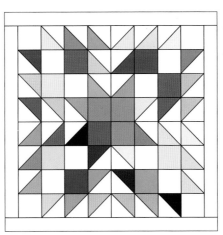

Quilt assembly

Materials

Assorted prints: ¾ yard total

White solid: 1⅜ yards

Backing: 1¼ yards

Binding: ⅜ yard

Batting: 40" × 40"

Cutting

See the tip (below) before cutting squares for half-square triangles.

Assorted prints:
- Cut 20 squares 4½" × 4½" for half-square triangles.
- Cut 12 squares 4" × 4" for blocks.

White solid:
- Cut 20 squares 4½" × 4½" for half-square triangles.
- Cut 12 squares 4" × 4" for blocks.
- Cut 4 strips 2½" × width of fabric for outer borders; cut the strips into 2 strips 2½" × 28½" and 2 strips 2½" × 32½".

Binding:
- Cut 4 strips, 2½" × width of fabric.

TIP

Using 20 different prints will give you 20 matching pairs of half-square triangles. For more variety, cut squares from additional fabrics and save the extra half-square triangles for another project, such as the Spring Flowers Pillow (page 52). I used 40 different prints in my quilt and had 40 leftover half-square triangles. The yardage given for the white fabric is enough to cut the extra background squares. If you don't want extras, 1 yard is enough.

Spring Flowers Pillow

Finished block: 3″ × 3″ • Finished pillow: 15″ × 15″

Fabrics: Simply Color by V & Co. for Moda and Cuzco by Kate Spain for Moda

Pieced by Sherri McConnell and quilted by Natalia Bonner

There is nothing that says modern, retro, and traditional all at the same time as well as the simple half-square triangle block. After the pillow was quilted, the combination of bright colors and loopy quilting reminded me of a spring flower garden.

Block Assembly

Refer to Quiltmaking Basics (page 74) as needed. Seam allowances are ¼″ unless otherwise noted.

1 Place a print 4″ × 4″ square with a white 4″ × 4″ square, right sides together, and make 16 half-square triangle blocks (page 75). Press the squares open and trim to 3½″ × 3½″.

Make 16.

2 Arrange the half-square triangles in 4 rows of 4 blocks each as shown in the pillow top assembly diagram.

3 Sew the blocks together in each row, pressing the seams open. Sew the rows together, and press the seams open.

4 Sew the 2½″ × 12½″ borders to the top and bottom sides of the pillow top. Press toward the border. Sew the 2½″ × 15½″ borders to the left and right sides of the pillow top. Press toward the border.

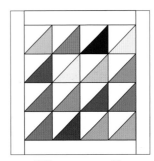

Pillow top assembly

Pillow Assembly

To complete the pillow, follow the instructions for Pillow Assembly, Steps 1–6 (page 29), for the Sugar Pine Pillow.

Materials

Assorted prints: ¼ yard total

White solid: ⅜ yard

Pillow back: ½ yard

Binding: ¼ yard

Muslin: ½ yard

Batting: 18″ × 18″

Pillow form: 15″ × 15″

Cutting

If you want more variety in your prints, cut additional white and print squares. Save leftover half-square triangles for another project.

Assorted prints:
- Cut 8 squares 4″ × 4″ for half-square triangles.

White solid:
- Cut 8 squares 4″ × 4″ for half-square triangles.
- Cut 2 strips 2″ × width of fabric; then cut 2 rectangles 2″ × 12½″ and 2 rectangles 2″ × 15½″ for outer border.

Pillow back fabric:
- Cut 1 square 15½″ × 15½″ and 1 rectangle 12″ × 15½″.`

Muslin:
- Cut 1 square 18″ × 18″.

Binding:
- Cut 2 strips 2¼″ × width of fabric.

The loopy quilting Natalia used in this pillow is the perfect way to let the fabrics do the talking. Loopy quilting is a technique that is easy for the beginner quilter to use in quilting small projects.

Groovy

Finished block: 12″ × 12″ • Finished quilt: 56″ × 70″

Fabrics: Gypsy Girl by Lily Ashbury for Moda

Pieced by Sherri McConnell and quilted by Natalia Bonner

Groovy started with a design in my sketchbook. I sketched it one way and then another, shading different areas light and dark and then reshading them in different patterns. I thought about making this block as a two-color quilt. Then I thought it would be fun to design the quilt with three fabrics plus a background in each block. When I saw the Gypsy Girl collection, I knew the fabrics would be perfect for this design, which seemed so classic and yet so today and, as a bonus, reminded me of the carefree days of summer.

Block Assembly

Refer to Quiltmaking Basics (page 74) as needed.
Seam allowances are ¼″ unless otherwise noted.

> ### TIP
>
> Before beginning, it's a good idea to pick out all the color combinations for each block. In the quilt shown, the corner squares and the Flying Geese units are made using one medium/dark print, the center square is another print fabric, and the rectangles and inner corners that create the ring are made from a third print.

1 Draw a diagonal line on the wrong side of 8 cream 2½″ × 2½″ squares. Place a marked square on a 2½″ × 4½″ rectangle, right sides together, as shown. Sew on the drawn line. Press toward the rectangle, and trim the seam to ¼″. Sew a second marked square on the other side of the print rectangle, right sides together. Press and trim. Make 4 matching Flying Geese units.

Sew.   Trim.   Press.

Make 4.

Materials

Assorted prints: 24 fat quarters

Cream solid: 2⅜ yards

Outer border: 1⅛ yards

Backing: 3⅝ yards

Binding: ⅝ yard

Batting: 64″ × 78″

Cutting

Assorted prints:
- From each of 12 different fat quarters cut:

  4 rectangles 2½″ × 4½″ for Flying Geese

  5 squares 4½″ × 4½″ for block corner squares and center square

- From each of the remaining 12 fat quarters cut:

  4 rectangles 2½″ × 4½″ for block "ring"

  4 squares 2½″ × 2½″ for block ring

- From the scraps of 20 fat quarters cut 1 square 2½″ × 2½″ from each (20 total) for sashing squares.

Cream solid:
- Cut 26 strips 2½″ × width of fabric; subcut into:

  240 squares 2½″ × 2½″ for blocks

  31 strips 2½″ × 12½″ for sashing

- Cut 6 strips 2″ × width of fabric. Piece for length, then cut into 2 strips 2″ × 58½″ for side inner borders and 2 strips 2″ × 47½″ for top and bottom inner borders.

Outer border:
- Cut 7 strips 5″ × width of fabric. Piece for length, then cut into 2 strips 5″ × 61½″ for left and right outer borders and 2 strips 5″ × 56½″ for top and bottom outer borders.

Binding:
- Cut 7 strips 2½″ × width of fabric.

> ### TIP
>
> If you make a lot of quilts with Flying Geese blocks (as I do), look into Monica Dillard's Fit to be Geese ruler at www.opengatequilts.com. It's an accurate way to make a lot of Flying Geese blocks.

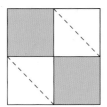 Draw a diagonal line on the wrong side of 4 print and 12 cream 2½˝ × 2½˝ squares. The print squares should be from a second print that will create the ring in the block.

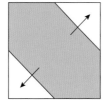 Sew 2 marked cream squares to opposite corners of a 4½˝ × 4½˝ print square by stitching on the drawn line. The 4½˝ print square should match the Flying Geese units from Step 1. Press toward the cream and trim the seam allowance to ¼˝.

Sew, trim, and press.

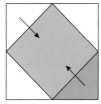 Sew a cream square and a print square to the remaining corners. Press toward the square and trim to make a square-in-a-square unit. Make 4.

Make 4.

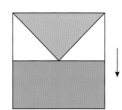 Sew each Flying Geese unit to a 2½˝ × 4½˝ print rectangle that matches the corner triangle of the unit from Step 4. Be sure to position the geese unit as shown in the diagram. Press toward the rectangle.

Sew Flying Geese unit to rectangle.

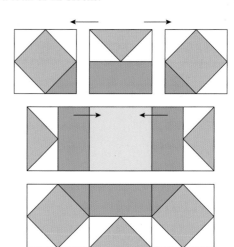 Arrange the units from Steps 4 and 5 around a 4½˝ center square from a third print as shown. Sew the units into rows. Press and sew the rows together. Press. Make a total of 12 blocks.

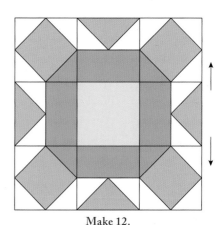

Make 12.

Quilt Assembly

1 Arrange the blocks, cream sashing strips, and assorted print sashing posts as shown in the quilt assembly diagram. Be sure you like the placement of the blocks and sashing squares and that the colors are distributed evenly throughout the quilt.

2 Sew the blocks together with 4 sashing strips to make a block row, beginning and ending each row with a sashing strip. Press toward the sashing strips. Make 4 rows.

3 Sew the 4 sashing squares and 3 sashing strips to make a sashing row. Press toward the sashing strips. Make 5 sashing rows.

4 Sew the rows together. Press toward the sashing rows.

5 Sew the cream 2˝ × 58½˝ inner border strips to the left and right sides of the quilt. Press toward the inner borders. Sew the 2˝ × 47½˝ inner border strips to the top and bottom of the quilt. Press toward the inner borders.

6 Sew the 5˝ × 61½˝ outer border strips to the left and right sides of the quilt. Press toward the outer border. Sew the 5˝ × 56½˝ outer border strips to the top and bottom of the quilt. Press toward the outer border.

7 Layer the backing, batting, and quilt top. Quilt as desired. Bind the edges (see Binding, page 77).

Quilt assembly

Sassy

Finished block: 10½″ × 10½″ • Finished quilt: 70½″ × 82½″

Fabrics: Happy Go Lucky by Bonnie & Camille for Moda fabrics

Pieced by Sherri McConnell and quilted by Andrea Marquez

This quilt is a lot of fun to make. It goes together quickly and can be made with one charm pack (5″ × 5″ squares), one roll of 2½″-wide precut strips such as jelly rolls, and some background fabric. The precut strips make cutting a breeze. The addition of white solid in the blocks and sashing really seems to make the precut fabrics sparkle. Use precuts from the same collection or mix and match collections for even more interest.

Block Assembly

Refer to Quiltmaking Basics (page 74) as needed. Seam allowances are ¼″ unless otherwise noted.

1 Sew white 1½″ × 5″ strips to the left and right sides of each 5″ × 5″ square. Press toward the white. Sew white 1½″ × 7″ strips to the top and bottom of each unit. Press toward the white.

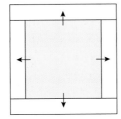

Sew white strips to square.

2 Sew 2 matching 2½″ × 7″ strips to the left and right sides of the unit from Step 1. Press toward the outer strips. Sew 2 matching 2½″ × 11″ strips to the top and bottom of the unit. Press toward the outer strips. Repeat the steps to make 42 blocks.

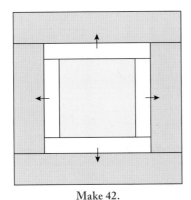

Make 42.

Materials

Assorted prints: 42 charm squares (5″ × 5″ squares) and 42 precut 2½″-wide strips* *or* use scraps

White solid: 2¾ yards

Backing: 5¼ yards

Binding: ⅔ yard

Batting: 79″ × 91″

* Note: Some precut rolls have only 40 strips, so it may be necessary to cut 2 extra strips from coordinating fabric. Extra yardage has been included with the backing fabric to cut these strips if needed.

Cutting

Assorted prints:

· Cut 42 squares 5″ × 5″ (if using scraps).

· From each 2½″ × width of fabric strip,* cut 2 strips 2½″ × 7″ and 2 strips 2½″ × 11″.

· Cut 30 squares 2″ × 2″ from leftover strip ends for sashing squares.

White solid:

· Cut 28 strips 1½″ × width of fabric; subcut into 84 strips 1½″ × 5″ and 84 strips 1½″ × 7″ for blocks.

· Cut 4 strips 11″ × width of fabric; subcut into 71 strips 2″ × 11″ for sashing.

Binding:

· Cut 8 strips 2½″ × width of fabric.

* If using scraps, cut the pieces in matching sets of 4, 2 of each length.

Inspiration Notebook

Keeping an inspiration or idea notebook is an excellent way to record all of your thoughts and notes about the different things that inspire you. I keep lists of patterns I want to make, color combinations I want to try out, and sketches of blocks I want to make. I also include quotations that I find inspiring. I look at magazines to find photos to add to this notebook, and I use colored pencils and pens to make notes. Today, Pinterest boards function as an online idea notebook and journal of the things we love. Not only can you record your ideas and inspirations on your various boards, but you have instant access to the boards of friends and family and artists and quilters whose work you admire.

Quilt Assembly

1 Arrange the blocks in 7 rows of 6 blocks each with white 2″ × 11″ sashing strips between blocks. Rearrange the blocks until you like the distribution of color and value.

2 Sew the blocks and sashing strips together into rows. Press toward the sashing.

3 Sew 6 white 2″ × 11″ sashing strips together with 5 sashing squares, beginning and ending the row with a sashing strip. Press toward the sashing strips. Make 6 rows.

Make 6.

4 Assemble the quilt by sewing together the block rows and the sashing rows.

5 Layer the backing, batting, and quilt top. Quilt as desired. Bind the edges (see Binding, page 77).

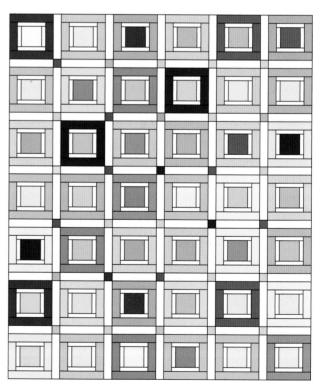

Quilt assembly

Garden Days

Finished block: 8″ × 8″ • Finished quilt: 60″ × 76″

Fabrics: Pam Kitty Love by Pam Vierra-McGinnis for Lakehouse Fabrics

Pieced by Sherri McConnell and quilted by Natalia Bonner

Materials

Assorted prints: 1 layer cake (42 squares 10″ × 10″) or 3⅛ yards total

White solid: 1¾ yards

Outer border: 1⅛ yards

Binding fabric: ⅔ yard

Backing: 4¾ yards

Batting: 68″ × 84″

Cutting

Assorted prints:

· From each layer cake (10″ × 10″) square or assorted fabrics, cut 2 strips 1½″ × 8½″ and 2 strips 1½″ × 6½″ (42 matching sets).

· From remaining layer cake squares or assorted fabrics, cut a total of 42 strips 2½″ × 10″ and 36 strips 1½″ × 6½″.

White solid:

· Cut 30 strips 1½″ × width of fabric; subcut into:

  12 strips 1½″ × 8½″ for blocks

  96 strips 1½″ × 6½″ for blocks

  84 strips 1½″ × 4½″ for blocks

· Cut 6 strips 2″ × width of fabric for inner border.

Outer border:

· Cut 7 strips 5″ × width of fabric for outer border.

Binding:

· Cut 8 strips 2½″ × width of fabric.

Layer cake squares (10″ × 10″) seem to be my precut of choice. They are wider than other precuts, allowing them to be used for a variety of block constructions. When I designed this quilt, I was trying to use one layer cake with little waste in order to make the biggest quilt possible. Cut carefully if using a single layer cake for this quilt. This quilt also makes a wonderful scrap quilt; just cut the strips and pieces from your scrap bin and have fun!

Block Assembly

Refer to Quiltmaking Basics (page 74) as needed. Seam allowances are ¼″ unless otherwise noted.

① Sew together 2 assorted print 2½″ × 10″ strips. Press toward the darker strip. Repeat to make 21 sets. Cut each strip set into 4 segments 2½″ × 4½″ for a total of 84.

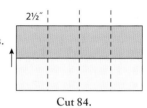

Cut 84.

② Join 2 different segments from Step 1 to make Four-Patch blocks. Make 42.

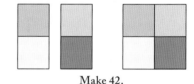

Make 42.

③ Sew the white 1½″ × 4½″ strips to the left and right sides of all the Four-Patch units from Step 2. Press toward the white strips. Sew the white 1½″ × 6½″ strips to the top and bottom of all the units. Press toward the white strips.

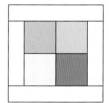

Add white strips.

4 Sew matching 1½″ × 6½″ strips to the left and right sides of the units from Step 3. Press toward the outer strips. Sew matching 1½″ × 8½″ strips to the top and bottom of the units. Press toward the outer strips. Blocks should now measure 8½″ × 8½″.

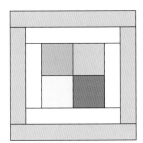

Make 42.

5 Sew together 6 different 1½″ × 6½″ print strips as shown to make a Rail Fence unit. Press the seams in one direction. Make 6.

Make 6.

6 Sew white 1½″ × 6½″ strips to the left and right sides of the units from Step 5. Press toward the white fabrics. Sew white 1½″ × 8½″ strips to the top and bottom. Press toward the white fabrics. Make 6 blocks.

Make 6.

Quilt Assembly

1 Arrange the blocks into 8 rows of 6 blocks each. Rotate every other block so that seams won't have to be aligned when sewing. Randomly place the Rail Fence–style blocks throughout the quilt top.

2 Sew the blocks in each row together. Alternate the pressing direction for each row so that the seams will nest when the rows are sewn together. Sew the rows together. Press seams in one direction.

3 Add 2″ × 64½″ inner border strips to the left and right sides of the quilt. Press toward the inner borders. Add 2″ × 51½″ inner border strips to the top and bottom of the quilt. Press toward the inner borders.

4 Add 5″ × 67½″ outer border strips to the left and right sides of the quilt. Press toward the outer borders. Add 5″ × 60½″ outer border strips to the top and bottom of the quilt. Press toward the outer borders.

5 Layer the backing, batting, and quilt top. Quilt as desired. Bind the edges (see Binding, page 77).

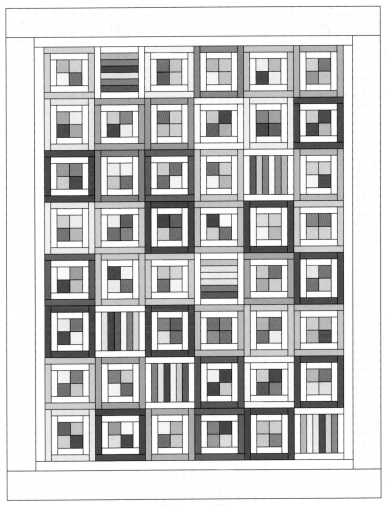

Quilt assembly

Breeze Pillow

Finished block: 12″ × 12″ • Finished pillow: 16″ × 16″

Fabrics: Lucy's Crab Shack by Sweetwater for Moda

Pieced and hand quilted by Sherri McConnell

I've always wanted to make this style of Dresden. With the straight edges and rounded outside, this block is classic and yet so modern, too! Nine of these blocks separated by patchwork sashing would make a stunning wall hanging!

Block Assembly

Refer to Quiltmaking Basics (page 74) as needed. Seam allowances are ¼˝ unless otherwise noted.

1 Sew the Dresden blades together in pairs. Press to one side. Sew the blade pairs together into a circle. Take extra care when sewing and pressing so that you don't stretch the bias edges.

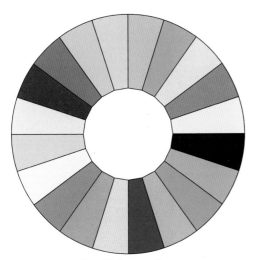

Sew blades together.

2 Spray a little of the spray starch into a small cup. With the paintbrush, paint the edges of the center circle with spray starch.

3 Using the tip of your iron or a small craft iron, press the edges of the circle over the freezer-paper template.

4 When cool, remove the template and press the circle again.

Materials

Assorted prints: 1 charm pack (5˝ × 5˝ squares) or ¾ yard total

White solid: ½ yard

Muslin: ½ yard

Pillow back: ⅝ yard

Binding: ¼ yard

Batting: 18˝ × 18˝

Pillow form: 16˝ × 16˝

Template material: Freezer paper for making templates

Other notions:

Spray starch

Small, inexpensive paintbrush

TIP

Instead of making your own freezer-paper templates, you can use the Easy Dresden tool by Darlene Zimmerman. It's a bit longer than the pattern provided, so you may need to trim extra fabric when pressing the freezer-paper circle to the Dresden plate in Step 7.

Cutting

Make your own templates (Making Freezer-Paper Templates, page 76) using the patterns (page 67), or use a purchased template.

Assorted prints:

· Cut 20 Dresden blades.

· Cut 1 center circle ¼˝ to ⅜˝ larger than the template on all sides.

· Cut 28 squares 2½˝ × 2½˝ for pillow border.

White solid:

· Cut 1 square 15˝ × 15˝.

Muslin:

· Cut 1 square 18˝ × 18˝.

Pillow back fabric:

· Cut 1 square 16½˝ × 16½˝ and 1 rectangle 14˝ × 16½˝.

Binding:

· Cut 2 strips 2¼˝ × width of fabric.

5 Appliqué (page 76) the center circle to the center of the Dresden circle.

6 Make a freezer-paper template as you did for the Dresden blade using the pattern for the outer circle (page 67). The circle should be 9¾″ diameter.

7 Center the large freezer-paper circle template on the wrong side of the Dresden circle. Press. Press the edges of the circle over the edges of freezer-paper template using the paintbrush and spray starch.

8 Center the Dresden on the background and appliqué it in place.

9 Trim the background square with the Dresden appliqué to 12½″ × 12½″.

10 Sew together the 2½″ × 2½″ squares into 2 strips of 6 squares each and 2 strips of 8 squares each. Press seam allowances in one direction.

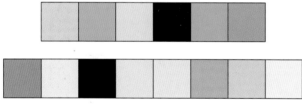

Make 2 of each.

11 Sew the 6-square strips to the left and right sides of the pillow top. Press toward the pillow.

12 Sew the 8-square strips to the top and bottom of the pillow top. Press toward the pillow.

13 Staystitch around all the edges of the pillow top using a ⅛″ seam.

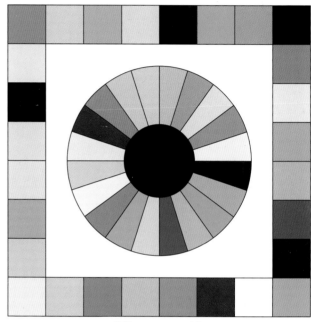

Pillow top assembly

Pillow Assembly

To complete the pillow, follow the instructions for Pillow Assembly, Steps 1–6 (page 29), for the Sugar Pine Pillow.

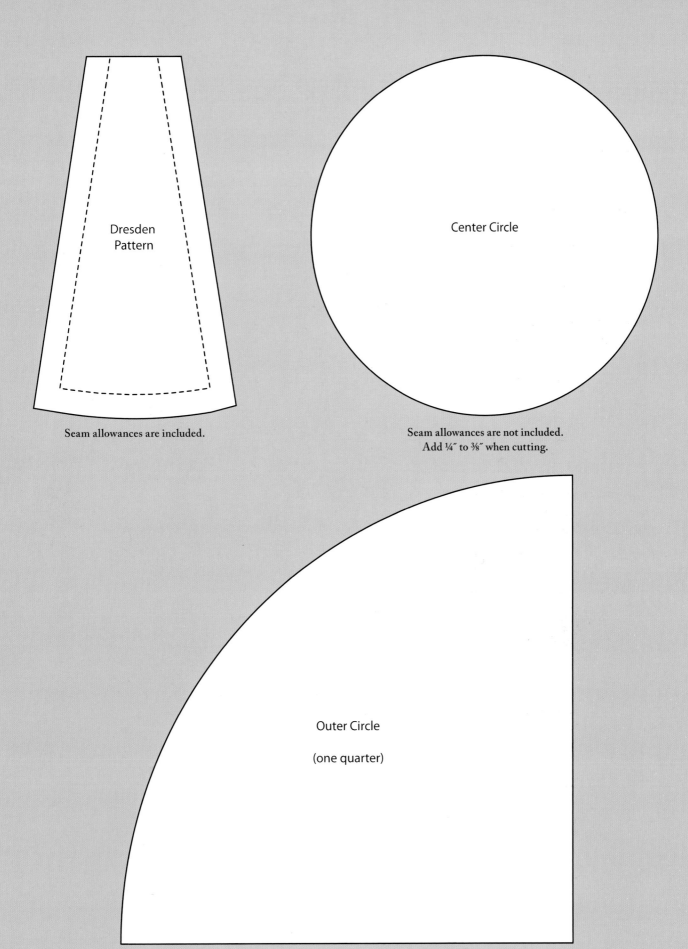

Dresden Pattern

Seam allowances are included.

Center Circle

Seam allowances are not included.
Add ¼˝ to ⅜˝ when cutting.

Outer Circle

(one quarter)

Flip pattern or trace 4 times to make complete circle.

Tumblers

Finished block: 6″ tall • Finished quilt: 57″ × 66″

Fabrics: 23 by Julie Comstock for Moda, assorted fabrics from author's stash,
and Moda Bella Solids in Gray

Pieced by Sherri McConnell and quilted by Natalia Bonner

I've been inspired by the Tumbler shape over the past couple of years. I've made several small projects, including Tumbler pot holders, Tumbler table mats, and Tumbler table runners. So it was definitely on my to-do list to make a larger Tumbler quilt. With this quilt I used a large Tumbler block. The quilt goes together quickly, and the Tumbler design gives it a polished look.

Quilt Assembly

1 Arrange the Tumbler blocks in 11 rows of 13 blocks each as shown in the quilt assembly diagram (page 70).

2 Sew the blocks together into rows. Alternate the pressing direction for each row so that the seams will nest when the rows are sewn together.

3 Sew the rows together, pressing the seams down or open.

4 Using a 24″ long ruler, draw a line along the left and right sides of the quilt using the narrowest points of the Tumblers on each side as a guide (refer to the trimming tip, page 41). Using a rotary cutter and ruler, cut along the drawn lines.

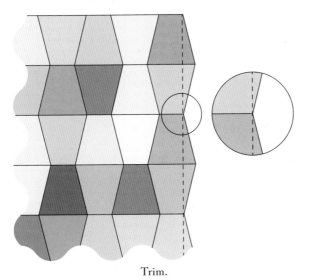

Trim.

Materials

Assorted prints and solids:
4 yards total

Binding: ⅝ yard

Backing: 3¾ yards

Batting: 65″ × 74″

Template material:
Stiff cardboard or template plastic

TIP

My favorite cardboard to use for templates is the heavyweight cardboard that comes on the bottom of layer cake precuts. I use a dull rotary cutter and an acrylic ruler to cut templates from cardboard. If you like to piece with more unusual shapes, you might consider the AccuQuilt Go! system. It has a die for Tumblers and will allow you to cut several pieces at once.

Cutting

Make your own template using the pattern (page 71).

Assorted prints and solids:
· Cut 143 Tumbler blocks.

Binding:
· Cut 7 strips 2½″ × width of fabric.

⑤ Staystitch ⅛″ from the outside edges to prevent stretching and fraying.

⑥ Layer the backing, batting, and quilt top. Quilt as desired. Bind the edges (see Binding, page 77).

Quilt assembly

Natalia used two different types of quilting to accent the Tumbler blocks in this quilt.
This is a wonderful idea to give extra interest to a quilt made up of one block type.

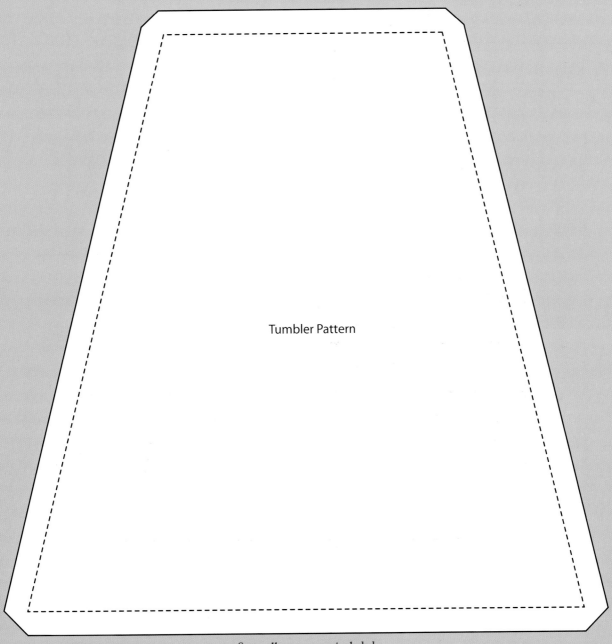

Tumbler Pattern

Seam allowances are included.

Boardwalk Runner

Finished block: 3˝ tall

Finished runner: 12¾˝ × 36˝

Fabrics: Avalon by Joanna Figueroa of Fig Tree & Company for Moda and Linen by French General for Moda

This smaller-sized Tumbler project is the perfect size for a table runner or even to set on a dresser top or kitchen counter. I made some small projects using these fabrics and fell in love with the combination of aqua, cream, beige, and red. Using solid linen for backing and binding seemed the perfect way to finish this project.

Pieced and quilted by Sherri McConnell

Quilt Assembly

1 Arrange the Tumbler blocks in 12 rows of 6 blocks each.

2 Sew the blocks together in each row. Alternate the pressing direction for each row so that the seams will nest when the rows are sewn together.

3 Sew the rows together, pressing the seams down or open.

4 Using a ruler, draw a line along the left and right sides of the quilt using the narrowest points on each side as a guide (refer to the trimming tip, page 41). Using a large rotary cutter, cut along the drawn lines.

5 Staystitch ⅛″ from the outside edges to prevent stretching and fraying.

6 Layer the backing, batting, and quilt top. Quilt as desired. Bind the edges (see Binding, page 77).

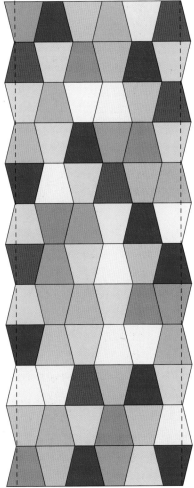

Trim.

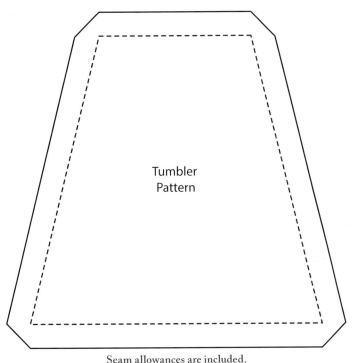

Tumbler
Pattern

Seam allowances are included.

Materials

Assorted prints: 1 yard total

Backing: ⅔ yard*

Binding: ⅓ yard

Batting: 21″ × 44″

Template material: Stiff cardboard, template plastic, or AccuQuilt Go! Cutter small Tumbler template

If your fabric is not 44″ wide, you'll need 1¼ yards.

Cutting

Make your own template using the pattern (bottom left), or use a purchased template.

Assorted prints:
· Cut 72 Tumbler blocks.

Binding:
· Cut 3 strips 2½″ × width of fabric.

> **TIP**
>
> There are a variety of acrylic Tumbler templates available. If you use one of those, you may see slight variations in the finished runner size. Miss Rosie's Quilt Company "The Crumbler" is one such template. Also, the AccuQuilt Go! Cutter has a small die that works for this design. Several Tumbler blocks can be cut at once using this cutter.

Quiltmaking Basics

Supplies and Tools

Every quilter needs a few basic items:

- **Pair of sharp scissors.** I prefer a lightweight pair.

- **Rotary-cutting tools:** a rotary cutter, self-healing rotary-cutting mat, and at least a couple of acrylic rulers. I find that I most often use the 6″ × 12″ and 8″ × 24″ rulers in my collection.

- **Sharp seam ripper.** Even though you always hope you won't have to use one, it seems I use mine frequently.

- **Glass-head pins** are another essential that you will use again and again. I keep my pins in a pincushion; it's easier to store and use the pins when you can easily take them in and out of the pincushion.

- **Iron.** I hadn't realized how important an iron is until a few months ago when my iron broke. It was readily apparent that I couldn't do very much sewing until I got a new one.

- **Fine-lead mechanical pencil.** This item is always in my sewing kit. I use it to mark lines when needed for half-square triangles and corner triangle units.

Of course, there are endless options for other gadgets, and I can honestly say it's a rare specialty tool or ruler that I don't love!

Cutting

One of the first things my grandmother taught me about quilting was an old adage that you are probably familiar with: "Measure twice and cut once." I remember repeating that in my mind when I first started quilting—I didn't want to waste any of the precious fabric I was working with. Even now, when I make a cutting error, it's usually because I haven't double-checked my measurements.

As for technique, always use a sharp rotary-cutting blade. It's also important to square up your fabric before you begin to cut.

Squaring Up Fabric

① Line up the bottom edge of the folded fabric with one of the lines on the mat to make sure the fabric is straight.

② Line up the ruler with lines on the mat at the top and bottom and make an even cut along the left edge of the fabric.

③ Repeat this squaring-up technique as often as needed, especially when cutting a number of strips or pieces from the same piece of fabric or if cutting pieces from layered fabrics.

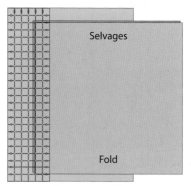

Squaring up fabric

> **TIP**
>
> When cutting strips, squares, and rectangles, use the lines on your acrylic ruler rather than the lines on the cutting mat. This will result in more accurate measurements.

The ¼″ Seam

An accurate ¼″ seam is a must in quilting. I have to admit that I pieced for several years before I learned a handy way to check the accuracy of my ¼″ seam. Most brands of machines have a special ¼″ foot available; however, it's important to measure your seam to make sure it is on target even when using one of these special attachments. Follow these steps to test your seam allowance.

1 Cut 3 strips of fabric 1½″ wide by 4″ or 5″ long.

2 Sew the strips together with your usual ¼″ seam allowance.

3 Press the seams to one side.

4 The middle strip should measure exactly 1″.

If your strip is too wide or too narrow, see if you can move your needle a little to the right or left to solve the problem. Another suggestion is to place a ruler under your presser foot and align the needle just a scant to the right of the ¼″ mark. Then use a few pieces of painter's tape to build up a guide with an edge. This will create a perfect ¼″ seam every time, and the painter's tape comes up easily if you need to move or remove it.

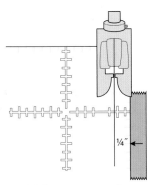

Making a seam guide

Pressing

In general, press seams toward the darker fabric. Press lightly in an up-and-down motion. Avoid using a very hot iron or overironing, which can distort shapes and blocks. Be especially careful when pressing bias edges, as they stretch easily.

Half-Square Triangles

To make half-square triangle units without actually cutting and sewing triangles, follow the steps below. I like to cut the squares slightly oversized and then trim the units after sewing and pressing. This results in perfectly square and perfectly sized units.

1 Place 2 squares of fabric right sides together.

2 Draw a diagonal line from corner to corner on the wrong side of the top square, or lighter square. Sew ¼″ away on both sides of the drawn line.

3 Cut on the drawn line. Press the seams open and trim. You will have 2 half-square triangle units. Specific sizes for trimming are provided in the project instructions.

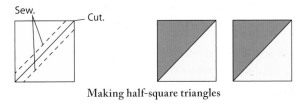

Making half-square triangles

Corner-Square Triangles

To make corner-square triangles, cut squares and rectangles as directed in the project instructions.

1 Draw a diagonal line from corner to corner on the wrong side of the smaller square.

2 Place the smaller marked square on top of the larger square or rectangle, right sides together, making sure the sides of the squares are aligned.

3 Sew a thread's width outside the drawn line (closer to the outside corner). Trim the seam allowance to ¼″ and press toward the corner.

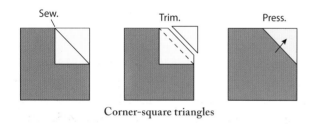

Corner-square triangles

Making Freezer-Paper Templates

I use a double layer of freezer paper when making templates so that the template is stronger and sturdier. This technique also allows me to use each template several times.

1 Trace the pattern onto the shiny side of freezer paper using a Sharpie or other permanent marker.

2 Cut out the shape ½″ outside of the drawn line.

3 Place the shiny side of the cutout shape on the dull side of another piece of freezer paper and press the 2 pieces together.

4 Cut out the shape on the drawn line.

You now have a double-layered freezer-paper template that can be ironed to your fabric. When ironing, make sure the shiny side of the template is against the wrong side of the fabric. Cut out the fabric ¼″ to ⅜″ outside the edges of the template to provide a turn-under allowance.

Appliqué Basics

While appliqué can be done by machine using an invisible stitch, I prefer to hand appliqué most of my work. Prepare the appliqué piece as directed in the project, turning the seam allowance under and pressing before positioning it on the background.

1 Place the piece to be appliquéd on top of the background fabric. Short appliqué pins may be used to secure your work, or you can use specially made water-soluble glues. If you use glue, place a small dot of glue every ½″ or so on the back of the appliqué piece, taking care to ensure that the glue is away from the very edge of the fabric, where you will be stitching. Roxanne Glue-Baste-It and Jill Finley's Appli-Glue are products that work well. When using pins, I prefer to use Clover appliqué pins, as they are sharp and easy to work with, and they are small enough to not get in the way.

2 To hand stitch, use a neutral-colored silk thread or a silk-finish cotton thread in a color that matches the piece to be appliquéd. Thread the needle and knot the thread.

3 Come up from the wrong side of the background fabric through the fabric to be appliquéd, very close to the turned-under edge of the appliqué piece.

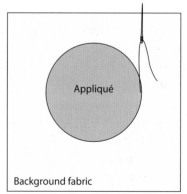

Bring the needle up through the appliqué.

4 Insert the needle straight down through the background fabric close to the edge of the appliqué and right next to where your needle came up.

5 Slide the needle about ⅛˝ and come up again through the background fabric and appliqué piece, catching just a few threads along the turned-under edge of the appliqué.

6 Repeat this stitch all around the appliqué piece until it is secured to the background fabric. All of the traveling stitches will be on the back of the fabric where they won't show, leaving just the tiny stitches on the front of your work.

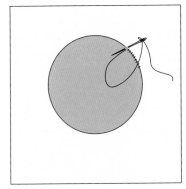

Stitch around appliqué.

Borders

In this section I've included a few tips concerning borders that will help you through the process while keeping your quilt squared up and easy for you or your longarm machine quilter to quilt.

Wait until the center of the quilt top is complete to cut the border strips to size. Always measure the length and width of your quilt through the center and compare the actual measurements of your quilt with the measurements given in the pattern. Pattern measurements are mathematical calculations based on an exact ¼˝ seam and don't take into account any stretching, bias, or differences in seam allowances. If your measurements differ, use the average measurement of the quilt at each side and at the center.

For borders that need to be pieced (longer than the width of your fabric), sew the border strips into one long length using a diagonal seam, to make the seam less noticeable. Because the border strips are sewn into one piece, the seams will end up in different places on the quilt, which also makes them less noticeable.

1 Place 2 strips together at a 90° angle, right sides together. Draw a diagonal line from the top left corner of the top strip to the bottom right corner of the bottom strip. Sew on this line. Trim the seam allowance to ¼˝. I press the seams open to reduce bulk.

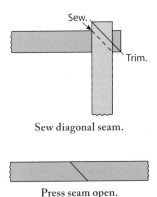

Sew diagonal seam.

Press seam open.

2 Pin the borders to the quilt top, easing as necessary to ensure that everything still matches up when you get to the end of the seam. Pin at each end, in the center, and at the midpoints between the two centers. The side borders are usually added first and then the top and bottom. Sew in the same direction when attaching the top and bottom borders and for any additional borders that you may need to add.

Backing

Unless you purchase extra-wide fabric for your quilt backings, most backings will need to be pieced. Seams may be pieced vertically or horizontally in order to best use the fabric available. Scrappy backs are a lot of fun to make, and it's a good way to use up extra fabrics from the front of your quilt. Whether you use a single fabric or several different pieces, be sure that your quilt backing measures 4˝ larger than your quilt top on all sides.

Binding

I nearly always use a double-fold binding that I stitch by machine to the front of the quilt, then fold over and stitch in place by hand to the back of the quilt.

I usually cut binding strips at 2¼˝, but many quilters cut them at 2½˝, so I've used that width in the cutting lists. Feel free to cut narrower strips if you prefer. For pillows, I kept the cutting at 2¼˝ wide strips. Occasionally I will use 2˝ strips if I want a very narrow binding.

Double-Fold Binding

1 Sew the binding strips together using a diagonal seam as shown in Borders (page 77).

2 Press the entire strip in half lengthwise with wrong sides together.

3 With raw edges even, pin the binding to the front edge of the quilt a few inches away from a corner. Begin sewing, using a ¼″ seam allowance, and leaving the first few inches of the binding unattached.

4 Stop ¼″ away from the first corner and backstitch one stitch. Lift the presser foot and raise the needle. Rotate the quilt one-quarter turn.

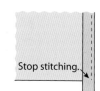

Stitch to ¼″ from corner.

5 Fold the binding up at a right angle so it extends straight above the quilt and the fold forms a 45° angle in the corner.

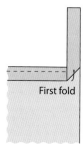

First fold for miter

6 Fold the binding strip down, even with the next edge of the quilt. Begin sewing at the folded edge. Repeat in the same manner at all corners.

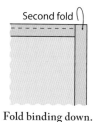

Fold binding down.

7 Continue stitching until you are back near the beginning of the binding strip. Fold under the beginning tail of the binding strip ¼″ so that the raw edge will be inside the binding after it is turned to the back of the quilt.

8 Place the end tail of the binding strip over the beginning folded end. Continue to attach the binding and stitch slightly beyond the starting stitches.

Note: You can also join the ends of the binding with a seam. See the tip at www.ctpub.com > Resources > Consumer Resources: Quiltmaking Basics > Quilting Tips: Completing a Binding with an Invisible Seam.

9 Trim the excess binding. Fold the binding over the raw edges to the quilt back, and hand stitch, mitering the corners.

> **TIP**
> I like to use Clover binding clips to keep the binding secure while I do the hand stitching.

Scrappy Binding

Scrappy bindings are a lot of fun to make, and they are the perfect solution if you forget to buy binding fabric with the rest of the fabric for your quilt.

For a scrappy binding, cut strips from scraps in assorted lengths. Join the strips on the diagonal until you have enough length for the binding. Sometimes I use scraps of one color, but at other times I've completely mixed up the colors.

> **TIP**
> Save leftover binding pieces from your quilts in a storage box. When you need or want a scrappy binding, go through the box and sew together pieces that coordinate. More than once, bindings created from leftovers have been the perfect ending for a project. Scrappy bindings are also fun to use with pot holders and pillows.

About the Author

Sherri is married and the mother of four children. She lives in rural southern Nevada with her husband. She received a bachelor of arts degree in English from the University of Nevada at Las Vegas in 1989 and teaches English part-time at a local community college campus. She spends as much of her free time as possible sewing and quilting.

Inspired by a rich family heritage of women who love sewing and creating, Sherri loves to sew and quilt. She has the most magical memories of homemade gifts from her mom, aunt, grandmother, and great-grandmother and began to sew on her own with a sewing machine at age ten. A patchwork pillow was her first project with a sewing machine, and she began sewing many of her own clothes during high school; as a college student and young mom, she sewed prom and wedding attire for others. In the early 1990s, encouraged and taught by her grandmother, she began her quilting journey. Just a few short years ago, she discovered quilt blogs and the amazing online community of quilters and their passion. Through blogging and creating, she has come to love designing and sharing this wonderful art. She has been publishing her designs in magazines and books since 2011; her first book, *A Quilting Life: Creating a Handmade Home*, was published in 2013. She continues to blog about her quilting life at www.aquiltinglife.com.

Also by Sherri McConnell

Resources

Appli-Glue by Jill Finley
www.jillilystudio.com

AccuQuilt
www.accuquilt.com

Clover Appliqué Pins and Binding Clips
www.clover-usa.com

Easy Dresden tool by Darlene Zimmerman
www.ezquilt.com

Karen Kay Buckley's Perfect Circles
www.karenkaybuckley.com

Marti Michell Perfect Patchwork Templates
www.frommarti.com

Great Titles *from* C&T PUBLISHING

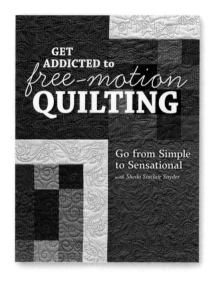

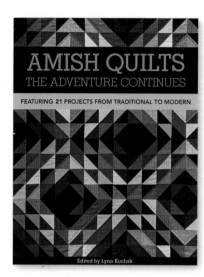

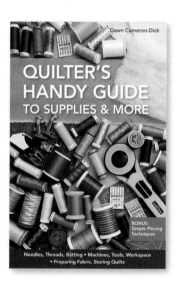

Available at your local retailer or **www.ctpub.com** *or* **800-284-1114**

For a list of other fine books from C&T Publishing, visit our website
to view our catalog online.

C&T PUBLISHING, INC.
P.O. Box 1456
Lafayette, CA 94549
800-284-1114

Email: ctinfo@ctpub.com
Website: www.ctpub.com

C&T Publishing's professional photography services are now available to
the public. Visit us at www.ctmediaservices.com.

Tips and Techniques can be found at www.ctpub.com > Consumer
Resources > Quiltmaking Basics: Tips & Techniques for Quiltmaking & More

For quilting supplies:

COTTON PATCH
1025 Brown Ave.
Lafayette, CA 94549
Store: 925-284-1177
Mail order: 925-283-7883

Email: CottonPa@aol.com
Website: www.quiltusa.com

Note: Fabrics shown may not be currently available, as fabric
manufacturers keep most fabrics in print for only a short time.